I0824877

BOOK CLUB
BAR

BOOK CLUB BAR

Literary-Inspired Drink Recipes *for Your* Next Great Read

ERIN NEARY & NAT ESTEN

Photography by SHENEUR MENAKER

EPIC INK

This book is dedicated to the many staff members, past and present, of Book Club Bar. You are the soul of the organization, and your dedication and creativity are what keep people coming back to our little shop.

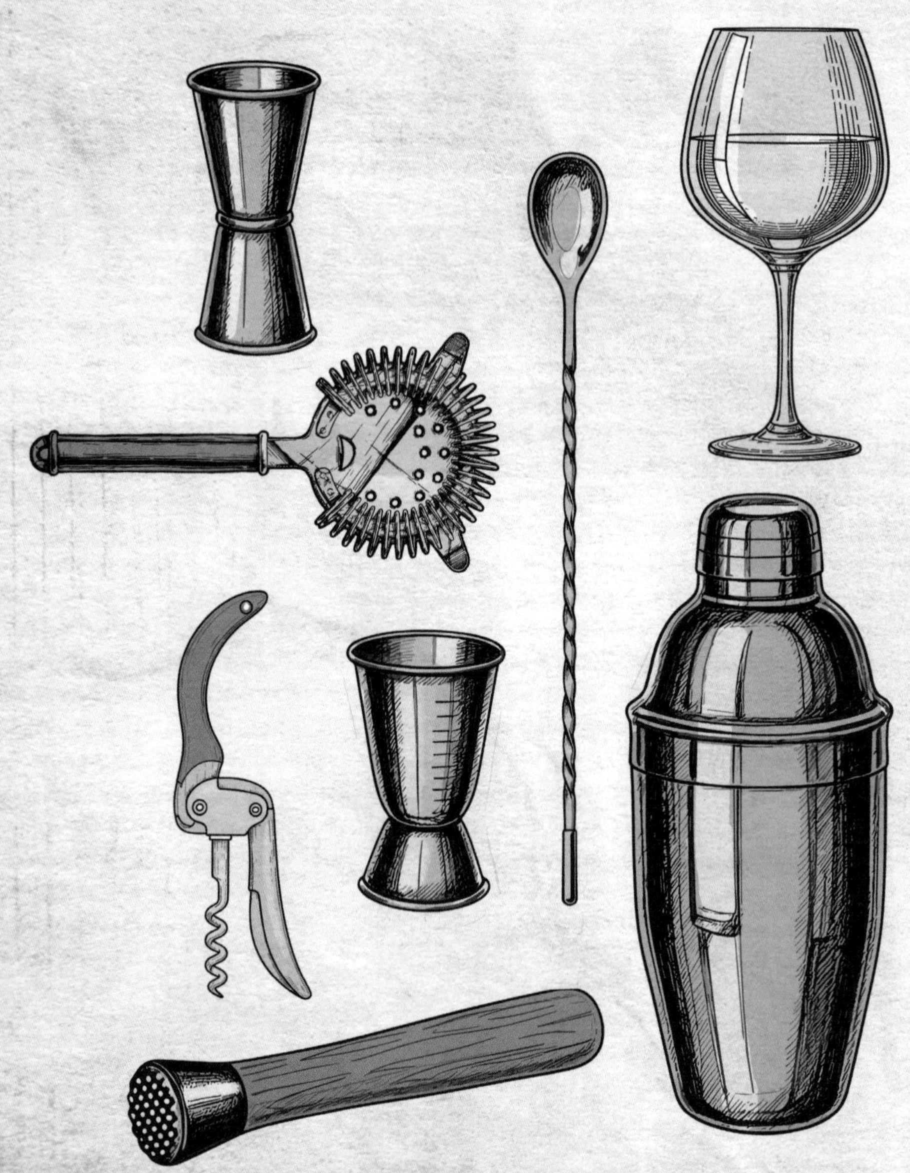

Contents

Introduction ✣ 10

Home Bar Recommendations ✣ 14

Book Club Bar Drinks ✣ 22

Crowd Favorites ✣ 24

A Gentleman in Moscow Mule ✣ 27

Author Spotlight: Amor Towles ✣ 28

Children of Blood and Virgin Mary (NA) ✣ 31

The Seven Husbands of Mary Pickford ✣ 33

It Ends with Citrus ✣ 35

Lessons In Chambord ✣ 37

A Thousand Splendid Rums ✣ 39

Author Spotlight: Khaled Hosseini ✣ 40

Mezcal Gothic ✣ 43

Where the Crawdads Bounce ✣ 45

The Godfather of the Woods ✣ 47

Happily Ever After ✣ 48

A Court of Fig and Honey ✣ 51

Author Spotlight: Sarah J. Maas ✣ 52

Lady Whistledown's Tea ✣ 55

One Italian Summer Spritz (NA) ✣ 57

Pearsuasian Martini ✣ 59

Author Spotlight: Jane Austen ✣ 60

Red, White & Royal Blueberry ✣ 63

Sex on the North Bear Shores Beach ✣ 65

Violet's Elixir ✣ 67

What a Thrill ⟡ 68

Murder on the Orient Espresso Martini ⟡ 71
Author Spotlight: Agatha Christie ⟡ 72
Dr. Frankenstein's Corpse Reviver No. 2 ⟡ 75
In Cold Bloody Mary ⟡ 77
Leave the World Behind ⟡ 79
Smoke & Mirrors ⟡ 81
Dirty Shirley Jackson ⟡ 83
Author Spotlight: Shirley Jackson ⟡ 84
Practically Magical Margarita ⟡ 87
Rosemary's Baby ⟡ 89
The Thursday Murder Mezcal Margarita ⟡ 91
Heathcliff's Ghost ⟡ 93

Literary Fiction ⟡ 94

A Virgin Suicide Shaker (NA) ⟡ 99
If Bourbon Street Could Talk ⟡ 101
Author Spotlight: James Baldwin ⟡ 102
Nightingale Nectar ⟡ 105
On Earth We're Briefly Sober (NA) ⟡ 107
Remarkably Bright Kraken ⟡ 109
The Handmaid's Cocktail ⟡ 111
Author Spotlight: Margaret Atwood ⟡ 112
Tomorrow, and Tomorrow, and Tequila ⟡ 115

Contemporary Classics ⟡ 116

Call Me by Your Nectar ⟡ 119
Donna Plum Tartt ⟡ 121
Author Spotlight: Donna Tartt ⟡ 122
Like Whiskey for Chocolate ⟡ 125
My Brilliant Ferrari ⟡ 127

No Country for Old Fashioned Men ✣ 129
Author Spotlight: Cormac McCarthy ✣ 130
The Cider House Mules ✣ 133
The Pineapple Rum Diary ✣ 135

Timeless Classics ✣ 136

The Deluge ✣ 139
De Beauvoir 75 ✣ 141
Author Spotlight: Simone de Beauvoir ✣ 142
Feminine Mezcal Mystique ✣ 145
Grapefruits of Wrath ✣ 147
Author Spotlight: John Steinbeck ✣ 148
Madame Boulevardier ✣ 151
Old Fashioned Man and the Sea ✣ 153
One Flew over the Cucumber's Nest ✣ 155
Picture of Dorian Earl Grey ✣ 157
The Sage of Innocence ✣ 159
Author Spotlight: Edith Wharton ✣ 160
The Tequila Sun Also Rises ✣ 163

How to Build a Book Club That Lasts ✣ 166
Book Club Models ✣ 168
How to Pick Your Book ✣ 170
Hosting and Theme Suggestions ✣ 172
Our Top 100 Book Club Picks ✣ 175
Index ✣ 182
Acknowledgments ✣ 189
About the Authors ✣ 191

INTRODUCTION

Book Club Bar is a bookstore and bar located at 197 East 3rd Street in the East Village of Manhattan. We first opened it in 2019, but our story begins long before.

We (Erin and Nat) first met in a book club in 2011. We argued over a book and made an instant connection and, eventually, got married. Both fans of reading in public spaces like bars and cafés, we dreamt of creating a space that would be a true hybrid of a neighborhood bar and an independent bookstore.

In 2017, we finalized our plan and began working toward opening Book Club Bar.

We officially opened our doors on Saturday, November 9, 2019. Still waiting for a beer and wine license, at first we only served coffee and tea with books. We had a few months of steadily building a reputation before the COVID-19 pandemic shut down the city. Forced to adapt, Nat delivered books to people in their homes while Erin served to-go drinks through our front doors. It was during these dark days that the store began to attract some of our most loyal regulars.

As the store built a following, we began hosting literary events. Author readings, book clubs, and educational talks filled the calendar. Eventually we hosted literary trivia nights, drawing classes, singles nights, acoustic music, holiday parties, and more. Our late hours allowed us to throw midnight release parties for highly anticipated books. These events helped bring new people to the shop and deepened our connection to the local community. A friendly and knowledgeable staff of "booktenders" kept people coming back.

In 2023, we were able to add spirits to our inventory, and it was finally possible to realize the dream of a full bar with literary-themed cocktails. Spearheaded by Lissa Bak, BCB's manager and head bartender, a new cocktail menu was conceived, and it rotates every season. Many of the cocktails in this book have been served at the bar, and some of them remain on the menu to this day.

As of the end of 2025, Book Club Bar is still thriving on 3rd Street. In 2026, we'll be opening our second location at 380 Troutman Street in Bushwick, Brooklyn.

Our passion has always been bringing people together to celebrate our love of literature, and we aim to create the perfect atmosphere for enjoying the literary world. Whether it be reading by yourself, sharing in a small book group, or taking in a big book event, Book Club Bar was designed to enhance and maximize that experience. Cocktails have always been a large part of that, and the goal of this book is to help you create your own literary community event.

Book Club Bar is a place in New York City, but if you enjoy the written word and cocktails (or mocktails), a spirited bookish affair is wherever you want it to be.

Cheers!
Erin and Nat

HOME BAR Recommendations

Home bars are built up over time. You'll snag a spirit for one style of drink and might not return to it for months. Some of the items required for recipes in this book you may already have, while others might be new to you. If you were to make every recipe in this book, here is what you will need. But don't get overwhelmed: We simplified and made these recipes easy to make at home, and many ingredients are found in multiple drinks. Each recipe makes one cocktail, so if you are making drinks for two, or for a group, the recipe can easily be multiplied.

GLASSWARE

Below are the styles of glassware used in this book. Glassware for particular cocktails are used depending on the ingredients or amount of ice used in the drink. Some of them are used out of tradition, which changes over time. For example, martinis were originally served in coupe glasses, then changed to the classic V-shaped glass, and now can be found in either. Here is what we recommend having on hand to build out your home bar glassware collection:

- Champagne flute
- Collins glass
- Copper mule mug
- Coupe glass
- Highball glass
- Irish coffee glass
- Martini glass
- Pint glass
- Rocks glass
- Wine glass

TOOLS

These tools are essential for making all standard cocktails. If you don't own any of the below, please add them to your shopping list!

JIGGER: This is used to measure, typically in ounces, any of the liquor, juices, or syrups used in your cocktails.

COCKTAIL SHAKER: A two-piece tool used to thoroughly blend ingredients. Some, but not all, have a built-in strainer on top.

HAWTHORNE STRAINER: Fits on top of a metal shaker and is used to separate liquid contents from ice. Use this if your cocktail shaker does not have a built-in strainer.

MIXING GLASS: Used to stir a mixed cocktail, such as an Old Fashioned, or martini.

OTHER TOOLS YOU'LL NEED

- Atomizer
- Coffee filter
- Small glass jars with lids (for simple syrups)
- Fruit peeler
- Kitchen twine
- Small pot
- Fine-mesh strainer (small)

STIRRING SPOON: Used to stir a mixed cocktail, or to add in an ingredient to a built (made directly in the glass) cocktail.

JULEP STRAINER: Fits inside a mixing glass to strain ice from a stirred drink.

TOOTHPICKS OR SKEWERS: Used to spear fruit, olives, or other cocktail garnishes.

INGREDIENTS

This list can look a little overwhelming, but it is simply the list of ingredients for everything contained in this book, and therefore it's what we usually have on hand at the bar. Each individual cocktail recipe will tell you exactly what you'll need to make it, so think of this as a high-level overview.

SPIRITS

These are your base ingredients for alcoholic cocktails. You'll likely recognize most of these names and each one has a distinct distillation process and flavor profile. Sometimes we'll use a specific brand if it fits the nature of the cocktail, but most of the time we'll use whatever the customer prefers. If you have your own favorite brands, feel free to switch them in!

- Bourbon
- Gin
- Sloe gin
- Mezcal
- Rum (Kraken Gold Spiced Rum)
- Rum (spiced)
- Rum (white)
- Rye whiskey
- Scotch
- Tequila
- Tequila (blanco)
- Vodka
- Vodka (cherry)
- Vodka (Stolichnaya)

LIQUEURS, FORTIFIED OR SPARKLING WINES

These are your secondary ingredients that will enhance a cocktail and make it more unique. In most cases, liqueurs (or cordials, as they're sometimes called) are lower ABV (alcohol by volume) than common spirits, but they're usually still very flavorful and aromatic.

- Absinthe
- Amaretto liqueur
- Amaro
- Blue curaçao
- Campari
- Chambord liqueur
- Cognac
- Drambuie liqueur
- Fernet-Branca
- Green Chartreuse liqueur
- Kahlúa or other coffee liqueur
- Maraschino liqueur
- Peach schnapps
- Prosecco
- St. Germain liqueur

- Triple sec
- Ume plum liqueur
- Vermouth, sweet
- Vermouth, dry
- Zirbenz pine liqueur

BITTERS

Bitters are flavor extracts steeped in alcohol and they are typically used in small quantities. They come in small specialty bottles, and as a quantity you'll see them employed in "dashes." These doses may be small, but they are powerful!

- Angostura bitters
- Aztec chocolate bitters
- Cardamom bitters
- Chocolate mole bitters
- Habanero bitters
- Orange bitters
- Peach bitters
- Peychaud's bitters
- Toasted almond bitters

JUICES

When it comes to lemon and lime juice, we prefer freshly squeezed. Any of the other juices found in this book can be sourced fresh or pre-made—it won't significantly affect the flavor of the cocktails.

- Lemon juice
- Lime juice
- Cranberry juice
- Grapefruit juice
- Orange juice
- Peach juice or nectar
- Pickle brine
- Pineapple juice
- Raspberry juice
- Tomato juice

SYRUPS

We have several recipes for homemade syrups throughout the book, but for the following flavors, we suggest store-bought (Monin or similar brand):

- Grenadine
- Lavender
- Maple
- Peach
- Pistachio
- Vanilla

HONEY

Honey aromas and flavors can vary—we're not picky, so pick a favorite! The cocktail may have a slightly different flavor each time you make it, depending on the honey.

COFFEE AND ESPRESSO BEANS

Most people don't have an espresso maker at home, so we suggest sourcing some fresh espresso from a local coffee shop. Two ounces is a "double shot" so you can order a number of shots based on how many cocktails you anticipate making. You can buy a small package of coffee beans for a garnish, and fresh grounds for an infusion.

FRUITS, VEGETABLES, AND HERBS

Fresh fruits, vegetables, and herbs are essential to the flavor and appearance of the cocktail. Doing your shopping the day of cocktail making will help ensure the freshness of the drink.

- Apples
- Basil
- Blackberries
- Blueberries
- Celery
- Cherry
- Cucumber
- Ginger
- Grapefruit

- Lemon
- Lime
- Mint
- Orange
- Pear
- Pineapple
- Rosemary
- Sage
- Strawberries

GARNISHES AND ADD-ONS

Our top three most commonly used garnishes are:

MARASCHINO CHERRIES: A preserved, sweetened cherry, typically jarred or bottled, that can easily be found in grocery stores.

OLIVES: Green olives, like Castelvetrano or Manzanilla, work best in martinis. You can play with the flavor of a cocktail by adding a blue cheese-stuffed olive, or pimento-stuffed olive, if you wish. Avoid black or olives packed in oil. *Note: It is an old superstition to serve a martini with an uneven number of olives—one or three olives is best!*

SODA WATER: Often interchangeably called sparkling water or seltzer—this is what makes a cocktail bubbly!

OTHER GARNISHES AND ADD-ONS

- Activated charcoal
- Apple cider
- Black pepper (cracked)
- Black pepper (ground)
- Blueberry tea
- Brown sugar
- Butterfly pea blossom flowers
- Cinnamon (ground)
- Cinnamon sticks
- Earl Grey tea
- Edible glitter
- Fee Foam
- Fig spread
- Frank's RedHot Sauce
- Ginger beer
- Horseradish
- Rock candy
- Rose water
- Sea salt
- Sesame oil
- Star anise pods
- Sugar
- Table salt
- Tabasco sauce
- Whipped cream (canned)
- Worcestershire Sauce

TECHNIQUES

Some basic techniques to master:

CHILLING GLASSES

Glasses can be chilled two ways: Putting them in the refrigerator for five to ten minutes ahead of cocktail shaking, or you can fill the glass with ice while you are preparing the rest of the ingredients. By the time you dump the ice and pour the contents, the glass should be good to go!

PREPPING VARIOUS FRUIT GARNISHES

- **Wheels:** Trim the fruit ends, then cut the fruit into rounds.
- **Slices:** Cut the fruit in half lengthwise, then cut a narrow strip of fruit.
- **Wedges:** Cut the fruit in half lengthwise and then cut the half into 3 to 4 wedges.
- **Twist:** Use a fruit peeler to get a narrow strip of fruit skin only.

ABSINTHE SPRTIZ

Use an atomizer or mister filled with absinthe for the absinthe spritz. Just a light spray of absinthe will add some flavor and smell to the cocktail, without overpowering it. If you don't have an atomizer, an absinthe rinse will do.

RINSING

A small amount of the liquor is added to a glass, swirled around the inside to coat it, and then discarded. The flavor and scent will remain in the cocktail, without overpowering it.

WHAT IS "A SPLASH"?

A splash is a bartender term for an imprecise quick pour of an ingredient. (Think just a quick flick of the wrist with a bottle—it will end up being about ¼ ounce or less.)

SHAKING A COCKTAIL SHAKER

Add the ingredients to the larger of the two shaker tins. Place the smaller piece on top and firmly seal. Hold the top and bottom of the shaker with each hand and shake vigorously over your shoulder for 15 to 30 seconds.

STIRRING A MIXED DRINK

To properly stir a martini or Old Fashioned, grip the stirring spoon between your thumb and first two fingers. Place the spoon along the wall of the mixing glass, nearly to the bottom of the glass, make a circular motion with your wrist, moving the spoon along the perimeter of the glass. Stir for about 30 seconds or until chilled.

BOOK CLUB BAR *Drinks*

When you walk into Book Club Bar in New York, the first thing you'll see is our long wooden bar on your right, probably with a bartender behind it shaking a drink. The next thing you might notice is our cocktail menu, which hangs over the bar and is usually placed throughout the store. This list is usually about six specialty cocktails, and it changes quarterly to match the vibe of the season.

We usually take into account what people like to drink in particular weather, national cocktail trends, popular books, and what our customers have been asking for. We will often bring back old favorites, and every season we try at least one brand-new idea. Of the six cocktails on our rotating menu, we tend to have at least one spirit-forward drink, something on the sweeter side, and one that's a little more tart or refreshing. That way there is something that will appeal to everyone!

As of publication, only one cocktail has appeared on every cocktail menu we've ever published: The Murder on the Orient Espresso Martini (page 71). This concoction combines two of the things we do best—a solid martini and delicious espresso.

Every cocktail in this book has appeared at our bar at one time or another. We are always tweaking and perfecting recipes, and there's always something new to try.

Crowd Favorites

As New Yorkers, we love to peek at book covers when we see people reading in public. (Since opening our own, we take note of which indie bookstore their bookmark is from!) On the subway, in the park, solo at a bar—catching a glimpse of a book cover or spine not only reveals a little something about the individual, but in aggregate, informs a zeitgeist moment for readers. In summer 2024, it was Miranda July's *All Fours*, and for years we've been seeing the red cover of *A Court of Thorns and Roses* (2015) by Sarah J. Maas *en masse*. In 2025, we saw dozens of New Yorkers reading *I Who Have Never Known Men* by Jaqueline Harpman, a reissued classic from 1995 that suddenly was everywhere.

What makes a crowd favorite? Often it is something that captures a cultural moment. For example, Khaled Hosseini's *The Kite Runner* (2003) and *A Thousand Splendid Suns* (2007) was, for many Americans, their first glimpse into the culture and history of Afghanistan, aside from what was being shown on the nightly news in the early 2000s. It sparked conversation and a deeper understanding of the conflict happening outside our borders.

Lessons in Chemistry (2022) and *Where the Crawdads Sing* (2018) were selections for celebrity book clubs, and subsequently spent week after week on top of the bestseller lists.

Crowd favorites, such as *A Gentleman in Moscow* (2016), can simply be summed up as books that are for everyone. There are characters to love, lessons to learn, and interesting stories to be told. They span genres and formats but are widely accessible and are sure to be a conversation starter.

A GENTLEMAN *in* MOSCOW MULE

A variation on the Moscow Mule, this spirit-forward cocktail uses ginger beer and lime juice to balance out the vodka and gin. Strong and refreshing, the perfect cocktail for long Russian winter days, or wherever you imbibe.

BOOK INSPIRATION

A Gentleman in Moscow by Amor Towles (2016). Alexander Rostov, a member of the Russian aristocracy, post-Revolution, is sentenced to life inside the Metropol Hotel, rather than a prison. The way he chooses to fill his time, and the people he meets inside, serve as a testament to the power of human connection despite unusual and often dire circumstances. While we know Count Rostov was a fan of fine wine, we think he would have appreciated this vesper-mule.

¾ ounce (22 ml) vodka (preferably Stolichnaya)

¾ ounce (22 ml) gin

½ ounce (15 ml) fresh lime juice

Ginger beer, for topping

Lime wheel, for garnishing

1. In a shaker filled with ice, combine the vodka, gin, and lime juice.
2. Cover and shake thoroughly until chilled.
3. Strain into a copper mule mug filled with ice.
4. Top with the ginger beer.
5. Garnish with the lime wheel.

AUTHOR SPOTLIGHT

Amor Towles

Amor Towles was born in 1964 and grew up in the Boston area before graduating from Yale University, and later from Stanford with an MA in English. A significant, early achievement was his thesis at Stanford, a short story called "The Temptations of Pleasure," which was published in 1989 in The Paris Review. He then moved to the Lower East Side of New York City in pursuit of a job and ended up working at a boutique investment firm; he stayed in that field for over 20 years before turning his focus to writing.

THE WORKS OF AMOR TOWLES (SO FAR)

In 2006, Towles gave himself a one-year deadline to complete his first novel. He finished the initial draft one year later, *Rules of Civility* was published in 2011 to great acclaim and became a *New York Times* bestseller. His works are emotionally rich and moving, with distinct worlds and characters you can't help caring about and have collectively sold more than eight million copies and have been translated into more than forty languages.

Rules of Civility (2011)
This 1930s-era New York City tale features a scrappy secretary from the Lower East Side as she becomes enveloped in the upper echelons of New York society and learns painful lessons along the way. Reviews often cite Towles's depiction of New York City wealth as reminiscent of Fitzgerald.

A Gentleman in Moscow (2016)
In post-Revolution Russia, a former member of the aristocracy finds himself confined for life to Moscow's Metropol Hotel. What starts as a bleak life sentence turns into a joyful exploration of friendship and chosen family.

ELITE BOOK CLUB PICKS

Each year President Barack Obama shares a curated list of his favorite books. The work of Amor Towles has graced Obama's list twice: in 2018 with *A Gentleman in Moscow* and in 2021 with *The Lincoln Highway*.

The Lincoln Highway (2022)
A road trip takes some extra detours and twists as Emmet Watson and his brother, Billy, accompany two friends from Nebraska to New York. Told from multiple perspectives over the course of ten days, readers are gripped by the characters, thinking of them long after putting the book down.

Table for Two (2024)
Towles's charming short story collection also includes a novella featuring Eve, the main character from *Rules of Civility*. Read that one before the novella for the intended impact.

BOOKSELLER'S MARGIN NOTE

We were first introduced to Amor Towles through Nat's mother, an avid reader, who told us we just had to read this charming story about 1930s NYC. She was referencing *Rules of Civility*, Amor Towles's first novel. We both fell in love with not only the book itself, but with Towles's particular brand of storytelling. His playful way with language often masks the gut punch to come. Towles quickly became an Esten-Neary household favorite.

One week after Book Club Bar opened in 2019, on Erin's birthday, Amor Towles himself walked into the store! For Erin, it was like seeing a celebrity. Author drop-ins have become more commonplace, but this was a first for us, and it was exciting. Amor has since become a friend of the store, and we've worked with him a few times on big stock signings for new releases. When we added a cocktail named after his second novel to our menu, he was delighted!

BARTENDER'S MARGIN NOTE

Batching Bloody Mary mix without vodka is great for a party or brunch gathering—and lets guests decide whether they want their cocktail to have alcohol or not. The vodka can always be added later (see our In Cold Bloody Mary recipe instructions on page 77).

CHILDREN *of* BLOOD *and* VIRGIN MARY (NA)

Tomi Adeyemi's afro-fantasy debut, *Children of Blood and Bone*, was an instant bestseller. While technically a young adult novel, we consider this accessible for adults as well. Given the all-ages factor of this book, we thought a virgin Bloody Mary was in order! It's a tasty nonalcoholic alternative to a cocktail. You'll notice this recipe is similar to the In Cold Bloody Mary recipe (page 77).

BOOK INSPIRATION

Children of Blood and Bone by Tomi Adeyemi (2018). The first in a planned trilogy, Adeyemi drew inspiration from fantasy classics, West African mythology, and the Yoruba people's language and culture. Set in the fictional country of Orïsha, presumed to be pre-colonial Nigeria, the people are divided into two groups: Divîners (possessing magic) and Kosidán (non-magical). King Saran, years before the events of the book started, disabled the magic and ordered the killing of many Divîners, including the mother of our protagonist, Zélie. She meets Princess Amari, daughter of the king, who has stolen the scroll which can restore the powers of the Divîner population.

4 ounces (120 ml) tomato juice

½ teaspoon prepared white horseradish

1½ teaspoons Frank's RedHot sauce

¾ teaspoon Worcestershire Sauce

¼ ounce (7 ml) fresh lemon juice

Pinch ground black pepper

2 green olives, for garnishing (optional)

Lemon wedge, for garnishing (optional)

½ stalk celery, for garnishing (optional)

1. In a mixing glass, combine the tomato juice, horseradish, hot sauce, Worcestershire Sauce, lemon juice, and pepper.
2. Stir thoroughly until flecks of pepper are distributed evenly throughout.
3. Pour into a highball glass or pint glass filled with ice.
4. Garnish with olives, a lemon wedge, or celery stalk.

The SEVEN HUSBANDS *of* MARY PICKFORD

The Mary Pickford is a classic Prohibition-era cocktail named for the Canadian-American film actress, who surely would have been a peer of Evelyn Hugo, were they to have existed in the same universe. Though Pickford was married to a measly three different men, she was a pioneer in the film industry and is considered to be one of the most important women in the history of cinema. This cocktail is a salute to both Evelyn Hugo and Mary Pickford, with a mixture of sweetness and spice that is a showstopper every time.

BOOK INSPIRATION

The Seven Husbands of Evelyn Hugo by Taylor Jenkins Reid (2017). A fictional Old Hollywood star, Evelyn Hugo, gives an interview comprising stories from her life, chronicled through each of her seven husbands. Each husband and relationship, recounted by choice descriptors (Goddamn Don Adler) is explored by Evelyn. Readers are surprised by the ending plot twist, when we learn the true love of Evelyn's life.

1½ ounces (45 ml) white rum

1½ ounces (45 ml) pineapple juice

1 teaspoon grenadine

6 drops maraschino liqueur

Habanero bitters

1. In a shaker filled with ice, combine the white rum, pineapple juice, grenadine, maraschino liqueur, and a few dashes of habanero bitters.
2. Cover and shake thoroughly until chilled.
3. Strain into a chilled coupe.

IT ENDS *with* CITRUS

Perhaps the finest classic citrus cocktail is a Southside, perfectly pairing gin, lime juice, and mint. The Southside itself is a riff on a Gimlet, but we put a further spin on it to pair with *It Ends with Us* by Colleen Hoover. The mint and lime are refreshing and crisp—perfect for a summer day. This drink can also be served on ice in a rocks glass, if requested.

BOOK INSPIRATION

It Ends with Us by Colleen Hoover (2016). Often mistakenly categorized as a romance novel, there's no classic "happily ever after" in this complex story of a physically and emotionally abusive relationship. Lily's vow to end a cycle of violence is ultimately a story of resilience and self-worth.

Mint Simple Syrup
(makes 12 ounces/360 ml)

1 cup (200 g) granulated sugar

½ cup (25 g) mint leaves, stems removed

8 ounces (240 ml) boiling water

Cocktail

2 ounces (60 ml) gin

1 ounce (30 ml) fresh lime juice

½ ounce (15 ml) Mint Simple Syrup

¼ ounce (7 ml) triple sec

Fresh mint leaves, for muddling and garnishing

1. **To make the mint simple syrup:** In a small pot, combine the sugar and mint leaves. Slowly add the hot water, stirring until the sugar is dissolved. Let steep for 2 hours. Strain through a fine-mesh strainer into a glass jar or airtight container. Let cool completely. Store in the refrigerator for up to 1 month.
2. **To make the cocktail:** In a shaker filled with ice, combine the gin, lime juice, mint syrup, triple sec, and four to five mint leaves (more if you prefer).
3. Cover and shake thoroughly until chilled.
4. Strain into a martini glass.
5. Garnish with a fresh mint sprig.

132
Oh sleep! it is
Beloved from
To Mary Queen the
She sent the gentle
That slid into my soul.
The silly buckets on the
That had so long remained,
I dreamt that they were filled
And when I awoke, it rained.
My lips were wet, my throat was cold,
My garments all were dank;
Sure I had drunken in my dreams,
And still my body drank.
I moved, and could not feel my limbs:
I was so light—almost
I thought that I had died in sleep,
And was a blessed ghost.
And soon I heard a roaring wind:
It did not come anear;
But with its sound it shook the sails,
That were so thin and sere.
The upper air burst into life!
And a hundred fire-flags sheen,
To and fro they were hurried about!
And to and fro, and in and out,
The wan stars danced between.

LESSONS *in* CHAMBORD

Mixology is a chemical science, so in a sense, all cocktails are lessons in chemistry. Inspired by *Lessons in Chemistry* by Bonnie Garmus, this cocktail is our version of a Bramble, a London dry gin spring cocktail, typically made with a blackberry liqueur. Our version uses Chambord to maintain the refreshing berry flavor. It is a drink whose balance of sweet and sour flavors mirrors Elizabeth's exercises as a chemist and a cooking show host. According to chemistry, alcohol is a solution!

BOOK INSPIRATION

Lessons in Chemistry by Bonnie Garmus (2022). In the 1960s, Elizabeth Zott is fired from the university where her career as a scientist is about to take off. Years later, she lands a TV cooking show, where she teaches women the science behind cooking and baking. Using science to teach housewives, she upends societal norms while navigating personal loss.

Simple Syrup
(makes 12 ounces/360 ml)

1 cup (200 g) granulated sugar

8 ounces (240 ml) boiling water

Cocktail

2 ounces (60 ml) sloe gin

1 ounce (30 ml) fresh lemon juice

½ ounce (15 ml) Chambord liqueur

¼ ounce (7 ml) Simple Syrup

Lemon half-wheel, for garnishing

2 to 4 fresh blackberries, for garnishing

1. **To make the simple syrup:** To a small pot, add the sugar. Slowly add the hot water, stirring until the sugar is dissolved. Let cool completely, then transfer to a glass jar or airtight container. Store in the refrigerator for up to 1 month.
2. **To make the cocktail:** In a shaker filled with ice, combine the sloe gin, lemon juice, Chambord liqueur, and simple syrup.
3. Cover and shake thoroughly until chilled.
4. Strain into a rocks glass filled with ice.
5. Garnish with the half-wheel of lemon and blackberries.

A THOUSAND SPLENDID RUMS

We liked the riff on the book title *A Thousand Splendid Suns* to highlight the wide variety of rums available: variations of dark, gold, aged, spiced, and white (used in this cocktail). The sweetness of the rum perfectly mixes with the vegetal green Chartreuse and lightly aromatic rose water.

BOOK INSPIRATION

A Thousand Splendid Suns by Khaled Hosseini (2007). Khaled Hosseini's second novel explores the complex role of women in Afghan society, set against the backdrop of the Soviet conflict and Taliban rule. Mariam is forced to marry a man from Kabul, and a decade later Laila is also courted and married to Mariam's husband. While the two women are initially resentful of each other, they ultimately form a mother-daughter-like bond as they face an abusive husband together.

1½ ounces (45 ml) white rum

¾ ounce (22 ml) fresh lime juice

¾ ounce (22 ml) green Chartreuse liqueur (see Bartender's Margin Note)

½ ounce (15 ml) pistachio syrup

½ ounce (15 ml) rose water

Lime wheel, for garnishing

1. In a shaker filled with ice, combine the rum, lime juice, green Chartreuse, pistachio syrup, and rose water.
2. Cover and shake thoroughly until chilled.
3. Strain into a rocks glass over ice.
4. Garnish with the lime wheel.

BARTENDER'S MARGIN NOTE

Chartreuse, green or yellow, is a liqueur that has been made by Carthusian monks in France since 1737. Its flavor is complex: often vegetal or minty, peppery or spicy, with hints of licorice. If you can't find green Chartreuse, as it is made in limited quantities, you can use a substitute like Centerbe or Génépy.

AUTHOR SPOTLIGHT

Khaled Hosseini

Khaled Hosseini, the eldest of five children, was born in Kabul, Afghanistan, in 1965. His father worked as a foreign diplomat, and his mother was a Persian language teacher. His childhood in Kabul was relatively privileged—he grew up in an upscale neighborhood and considered it to be a thriving city. His family moved between Iran, Kabul, and Paris for his father's work with the Embassy of Afghanistan. They were in Paris in 1978 when the Saur Revolution took place. Two years later, with the start of the Soviet-Afghan War, they were unable to return to Kabul. The family applied for political asylum in the United States and settled in San Jose, California. Hosseini arrived at fifteen, unable to speak English. Despite the initial culture shock, he adjusted and ended up attending Santa Clara University and went on to medical school at University of California San Diego. He practiced as a physician in internal medicine for over a decade.

THE WORKS OF KHALED HOSSEINI (SO FAR)

Hosseini began writing his first novel in 2001, while still practicing medicine. *The Kite Runner* was published in 2003. The book was a bestseller, with over a million copies sold within the first two years, translated into forty-two languages, and has had a film adaptation. His subsequent novels received similar acclaim and his works have been published in over seventy countries and sold more than 40 million copies worldwide.

The Kite Runner (2003)

Set in Afghanistan, the novel explores a young boy's upbringing from the fall of the monarchy to the collapse of the Taliban regime. It deals with the survivor's guilt the protagonist feels, mirroring Hosseini's own experience of being able to escape during the Soviet war while others who were left behind suffered.

A Thousand Splendid Suns (2007)

This novel explores the complicated relationship between two Afghani women, married to the same abusive man. In contrast to the "father-son" story in *The Kite Runner*, this is often considered a "mother-daughter" story.

And the Mountains Echoed (2013)
A change in format from his first two novels, this book features interwoven short stories, each told from the perspective of a different character.

Sea Prayer (2018)
A short, illustrated novel focusing on the Syrian refugee crisis, within a larger context of immigration and displaced populations.

KHALED HOSSEIN'S HUMANITARIAN WORK

Outside the pages of his novels, Hosseini has taken up advocacy for refugees as a principal cause of his life's work. In 2006, he was appointed a UNHCR (United Nations High Commissioner for Refugees) Goodwill Ambassador. The UNHCR, is a mission-driven branch of the United Nations, with the expressed goal of protecting the rights and saving lives of refugees, displaced individuals, and stateless people. Its Goodwill Ambassadors are recognizable, public faces that spread the word of UNHCR work worldwide.

As one of UNHCR's longest-standing Goodwill Ambassadors, two decades of work has brought Hosseini on field visits to Afghanistan, Lebanon, Italy, Uganda, Jordan, Chad, and Iraq. He has been a key fundraiser for the organization's work, including their "Culture Collective," supporting works of film, music, and other art produced by refugees. The author proceeds from *Sea Prayer*, benefitted the UNHCR and his own Khaled Hosseini Foundation, which supports women and children in Afghanistan.

MEZCAL GOTHIC

Beverages distilled from fermented agave have ancient roots in pre-colonial Mexico, and mezcal's smoky, earthy quality has been a signature flavor of the region for hundreds of years. When creating a cocktail to match the tone of Silvia Moreno-Garcia's *Mexican Gothic*, mezcal was the obvious choice for a spirit, but to match its macabre undertones, activated charcoal makes for a libation as dark as the heart of the story's antagonist, Howard Doyle. Throw in a little spice and lime and you've got a delicious, spirit-forward drink that will make you feel the Mexican heat, even if you're in a creepy old mansion.

BOOK INSPIRATION

Mexican Gothic by Silvia Moreno-Garcia (2020). Mexican socialite Noemí receives a disturbing letter from her cousin Catalina and goes to be with her at their family mansion, High Place. What she uncovers unfurls within a hallucinatory fever dream of ghosts, eugenics, and a mysterious fungus spreading within the mansion's walls.

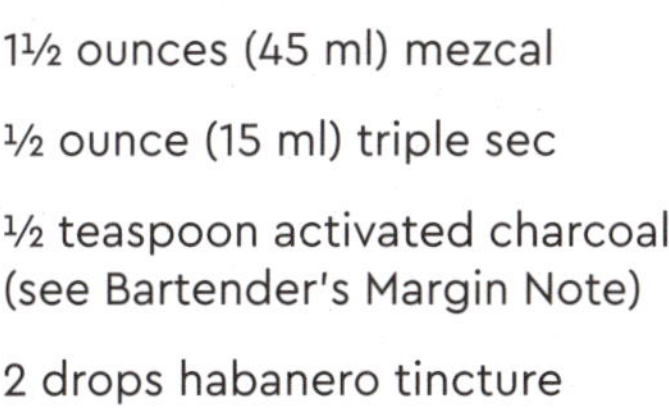

1½ ounces (45 ml) mezcal

½ ounce (15 ml) triple sec

½ teaspoon activated charcoal (see Bartender's Margin Note)

2 drops habanero tincture

Lime wedge, for garnishing

1. In a shaker filled with ice, combine the mezcal, triple sec, activated charcoal, and habanero tincture.
2. Cover and shake thoroughly until chilled.
3. Strain into a rocks glass filled with ice.
4. Garnish with the lime wedge.

BARTENDER'S MARGIN NOTE

Activated charcoal is flavorless and does not interfere with the taste of the cocktail. A small amount goes a long way to darkening the color of the drink! However, activated charcoal has a high absorption rate and can interfere with oral medications. If you wish to opt out of activated charcoal for this cocktail, you could replace it with a small amount of squid ink or black food dye to obtain the dark color of the drink.

WHERE *the* CRAWDADS BOUNCE

The unofficial cocktail of North Carolina is the Cherry Bounce, and it predates the capital city of Raleigh. When we were looking for a cocktail to pair with *Where the Crawdads Sing* by Delia Owens, set in North Carolina, the Cherry Bounce seemed like a natural fit. The recipe we found was from Martha Washington (yes, *that* Martha Washington), so we had to update it a bit. Sweet yet refreshing, this take on a Southern classic will have you bouncing in no time.

BOOK INSPIRATION

Where the Crawdads Sing by Delia Owens (2018). This dual-timeline story follows Kya, a young girl largely abandoned by a mentally ill mother, father, and older siblings, as she is left essentially to fend for herself in the marshes of North Carolina. In a second timeline, young adult Kya is being tried for the murder of a man who attempted to assault her. The story's crime element is woven in between a tale of survival and nature.

1½ ounces (45 ml) cherry vodka

2 ounces (60 ml) cranberry juice

½ ounce (15 ml) fresh lime juice

Soda water, for topping

3 maraschino cherries, skewered, for garnishing

1. In a shaker filled with ice, combine the cherry vodka, cranberry juice, and lime juice.
2. Cover and shake thoroughly until chilled.
3. Strain into a Collins glass filled with ice.
4. Top with the soda water.
5. Garnish with the cherries.

The GODFATHER *of the* WOODS

This cocktail is a twist on a traditional Godfather drink, a classic '70s-era Scotch and amaretto combo that often was used as an after-dinner drink or nightcap. We added a pine liqueur to connect the cocktail to the Adirondack setting of *The God of the Woods*, an essential element in the plot of the story. Sit with this one and allow the woodsy profile to be revealed—a drink surely to be served at the Blackfly Goodbye!

BOOK INSPIRATION

The God of the Woods by Liz Moore (2024). When a teen girl goes missing overnight at a sleepaway summer camp in the Adirondacks, the camp staff and town are reminded of a previous disappearance a decade earlier, the girl's older brother, and son of the wealthy camp owners. Readers, along with the local deputy, piece together clues and uncover family secrets about the two disappearances between multiple timelines.

1½ ounce (45 ml) Scotch

½ ounce (15 ml) amaretto liqueur

½ ounce (15 ml) Zirbenz pine liqueur (see Bartender's Margin Note)

Fresh rosemary sprig, for garnishing

1. In a shaker filled with ice, combine the Scotch, amaretto liqueur, and pine liqueur.
2. Cover and shake thoroughly until chilled.
3. Strain into a rocks glass filled with ice.
4. Garnish with the rosemary sprig.

BARTENDER'S MARGIN NOTE

Zirbenz is a brand of stone pine liqueur manufactured in the Austrian alps. When the cones are harvested mid-summer, they are full of sap, then soaked in grain brandy. Pine liqueurs are commonly used in après-ski gatherings. If you can't find Zirbenz specifically, you can substitute another pine liqueur, such as Brovo Douglas Fir, Pernot's Sapins liqueur, or Faccia Brutto Amaro Alpino liqueur.

Happily Ever After

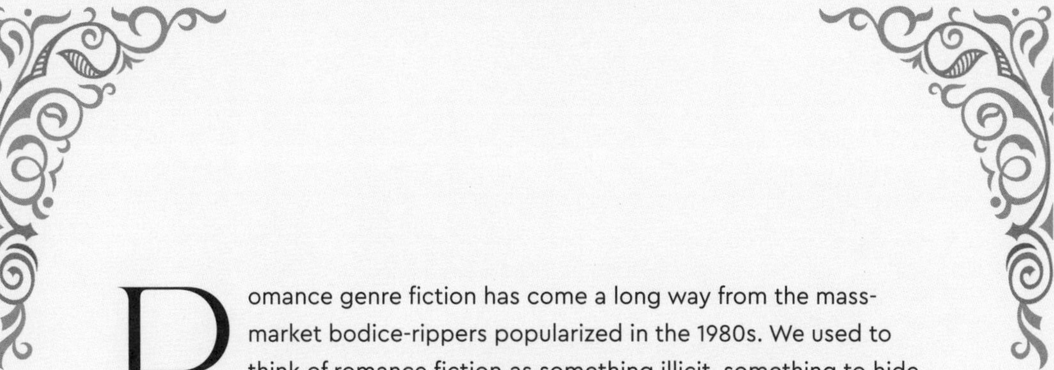

Romance genre fiction has come a long way from the mass-market bodice-rippers popularized in the 1980s. We used to think of romance fiction as something illicit, something to hide behind a "real" book, something to be embarrassed by.

Well, no more!

Romance genre fiction has skyrocketed in popularity in the last decade. As booksellers, we know that the numbers are off the charts and publishers are taking this type of fiction, and its readers, seriously. Around the country, romance readers have been emboldened by a found community on #booktok and #bookstagram and are pronouncing their readership loud and proud. No longer does romance fiction need to be sidelined.

What makes a modern romance? Many of the traditional romance tropes are still here (enemies-to-lovers, forbidden love, fake dating, and office romance), but with a modern twist. These are explored through social media, podcasting, and sports, to name a few settings. We have romances representing the spectrum of sexuality, neurodivergence, and race.

Of course, for a complete break from reality, newfound attention is being paid to historical romances and the wildly popular romantasy subgenre. Books like *A Court of Thorns and Roses* (2015) and *Fourth Wing* (2023) have resonated with readers yearning for an escape. The Bridgerton series has transported readers back to the Regency-era for classic romance with a historic twist.

Bottom line: We're all just here for a happily ever after, in whatever form.

A COURT of FIG and HONEY

This cocktail uses gin and amaro, a bittersweet and herbal combo. The addition of fig and honey syrup adds a warming richness and sweetness that balances out the other spirits, leaving you with a cocktail that's cozy and easy to drink.

BOOK INSPIRATION

A Court of Thorns and Roses by Sarah J. Maas (2015). The first of the A Court of Thornes and Roses fantasy series, nicknamed ACOTAR by fans, explores the faerie lands of Prythian. Feyre, a teenage huntress, is taken captive by Tamlin. What begins as a hostile situation evolves into a passionate love affair, as Feyre learns more about the faerie world and the threats it faces.

Fig and Honey Syrup
(makes 12 ounces/360 ml)

6 ounces (180 ml) honey

6 ounces (180 ml) fig spread

8 ounces (240 ml) boiling water

Cocktail

¾ ounce (22 ml) gin

¾ ounce (22 ml) amaro

¾ ounce (22 ml) Fig and Honey Syrup

¾ ounce (22 ml) fresh lemon juice

Lemon twist, for garnishing

1. **To make the fig and honey syrup:** In a small pot, combine the honey and fig spread. Slowly add the hot water, stirring until dissolved. Strain through a fine-mesh sieve into a glass jar or airtight container. Let cool completely. Store in the refrigerator for up to 2 weeks.
2. **To make the cocktail:** In a shaker filled with ice, combine the gin, amaro, fig and honey syrup, and lemon juice.
3. Cover and shake thoroughly until chilled.
4. Strain into a chilled martini glass or coupe.
5. Garnish with the lemon twist.

AUTHOR SPOTLIGHT

Sarah J. Maas

Sarah J. Maas, born in New York City in 1986, began working on her first novel, *Throne of Glass*, at age sixteen. She initially published parts of the story online before pulling it to be published through traditional channels. Her novels have sold over seventy million copies worldwide and have been translated into thirty-eight languages.

THE SARAH J. MAAS UNIVERSE: WHERE TO START

Subject of much debate online is which Sarah J. Mass series to read, and in which order. While not explicitly connected, the three series contain Easter eggs, and some outright spoilers of other books. Here's the order we suggest:

1. THRONE OF GLASS SERIES

This series skews YA, so it might not be for everyone. There are elements of the broader universe in here, but if you were to skip it and just go straight to the ACOTAR series, that would work too!

Throne of Glass (2012)
Crown of Midnight (2013)
The Assassin's Blade (2014)
Heir of Fire (2014)
Queen of Shadows (2015)
Empire of Storms (2016)
Tower of Dawn (2017)
Kingdom of Ash (2018)

2. A COURT OF THORNS AND ROSES SERIES

Read this before the Crescent City series. Many readers say this is the one that will get you hooked!

A Court of Thorns and Roses (2015)
A Court of Mist and Fury (2016)
A Court of Wings and Ruin (2017)
A Court of Frost and Starlight (2018)
A Court of Silver Flames (2021)

3. CRESCENT CITY SERIES

This series, a more adult fantasy story, contains some spoilers to the ACOTAR series, so it's safest to read this one last.

House of Earth and Blood (2020)
House of Sky and Breath (2022)
House of Flame and Shadow (2024)

BOOKSELLER'S MARGIN NOTE

One thing we love to do at Book Club Bar is host a midnight release party for a hot new book. The romantasy readers always show up with enthusiasm. In January 2024, we were in the process of planning a party for *House of Flame and Shadow*, by Sarah J. Maas (the third book of the Cresent City series), when we got a call from her publicist, saying that the author herself wanted to do a surprise drop-in at our event. We knew the fans would be in for a night to remember! No one knew but Book Club Bar staff, so when she unceremoniously walked through the front door, and attendees realized who was in their midst, it was a wild surprise. She graciously took photos with fans and answered questions, and everyone was that much more enthusiastic to walk out the door with her book at midnight!

Lady Whistledown's TEA

Lady Whistledown's gossip column serves all the tea, and what could be more appropriate than a tea-inspired cocktail? The warm citrus is calming, but the spiced rum and Tabasco are energizing. This fiery hot toddy will warm your insides and keep you cozy for a night in with *Bridgerton*.

BOOK INSPIRATION

The Duke and I by Julia Quinn (2000). Each book in the Bridgerton series follows a different sibling from the Bridgerton family, the first being Daphne, the oldest daughter. Daphne and Simon undergo a fake courtship, to ward off her other suitors, and fall in love in the process. The happily ever after comes later, after some controversial twists and turns (no spoilers!).

2 ounces (60 ml) spiced rum

6 ounces (180 ml) hot water

½ ounce (15 ml) fresh lemon juice

1 tablespoon honey

4 dashes Tabasco

Lemon wedge, for garnishing

1. In a coffee mug or Irish coffee glass, combine the spiced rum, hot water, lemon juice, honey, and Tabasco.
2. Stir thoroughly until combined.
3. Garnish with the lemon wedge.

BOOKSELLER'S MARGIN NOTE

Regency romance novels are a distinct subgenre of romance fiction, and a world unto themselves. Defined by the British Regency period of the early nineteenth century (1811–1820), they typically feature sharp banter and fast-paced dialogue between intelligent protagonists. Some Regency models follow the "Traditional Regency" standard, which is noted to be full of historical detail and sticks to the tone of the period. Other Regency historicals portray characters of the period with more modern values. Julia Quinn's The Duke and I *(2000), from the Bridgerton series, falls into the latter category, with more modern storytelling and explicit sexual content.*

One ITALIAN SUMMER SPRITZ (NA)

The book *One Italian Summer* by Rebecca Serle, with its sun-drenched setting, pairs perfectly with this nonalcoholic take on an Aperol spritz. Its bright colors evoke the sights and sounds of the Amalfi Coast, where the book is set, and its refreshing, sweet flavors make it the perfect complement to a beach read like this one. This pairing is best enjoyed in an al fresco environment.

BOOK INSPIRATION

One Italian Summer by Rebecca Serle (2022). This is not a traditional romance novel, but it's a great love story about a mother and daughter. When Katy is devastated by her mother Carol's sudden death, she moves forward with their planned mother-daughter trip to Positano, Italy. There, she miraculously finds her mother at thirty, alive and vibrant. The two are able to connect, and Katy learns so much more about her mother than she previously understood.

1½ ounces (45 ml) orange juice

1½ ounces (45 ml) grapefruit juice

Splash fresh lemon juice

Soda water, for topping

Orange slice, for garnishing

Basil leaf, for garnishing

1. To a wine glass filled with ice, add the orange juice, grapefruit juice, and a splash of lemon juice.
2. Stir until combined.
3. Top with the soda water.
4. Garnish with the orange slice and basil leaf.

PEARSUASIAN MARTINI

Martinis are a notoriously spirit-forward cocktail, one that people often shy away from if they don't care for the taste of vodka or gin. People are often intimidated by them—Dry? Dirty? Olives? While martinis as we know them came long after the Regency era, we like to think the women of Jane Austen's world would have enjoyed our twist on a martini, with pear-infused vodka, St. Germain, and lemon juice: simple, easy to drink, crisp, and refreshing.

BOOK INSPIRATION

Persuasion by Jane Austen (1817). This may be one of the earliest documented uses of the "second chances" romance trope. Anne Elliot, having broken off her engagement to Captain Wentworth seven years prior, is now considered past her prime at age twenty-seven. Wentworth comes back into Anne's life as a tenant on the Elliot estate, and the two find themselves in love once more. Close readers of Austen praise the book's modernity. It was Austen's final novel, published after her death at age forty-one, and many consider it to be one of her most mature works.

Pear-Infused Vodka
(makes 750 ml)

2 medium ripe pears, cored and sliced

1 bottle (750 ml) vodka

Cocktail

2 ounces (60 ml) Pear-Infused Vodka

¾ ounce (22 ml) St. Germain liqueur

½ ounce (15 ml) fresh lemon juice

Pear slice, for garnishing

1. **To make the pear-infused vodka:** In a pitcher, combine the pears and vodka. Let infuse at room temperature for 4 to 7 days, depending on your desired strength for the pear flavor. Strain through a fine-mesh strainer into a glass jar or airtight container. Store in the refrigerator for up to 3 months. (See Bartender's Margin Note.)
2. **To make the cocktail:** In a shaker filled with ice, combine the vodka, St. Germain, and lemon juice.
3. Cover and shake thoroughly until chilled.
4. Strain into a chilled martini glass or coupe.
5. Garnish with the pear slice.

BARTENDER'S MARGIN NOTE

This infused vodka recipe can be adapted, so feel free to play around with other fruit infusions! Alternatively, you can buy a pear-flavored vodka, such as Grey Goose La Poire.

AUTHOR SPOTLIGHT

Jane Austen

Jane Austen was born in 1775 in Steventon, Hampshire, England, to George and Cassandra Austen. She was the seventh of eight children. George and Cassandra, while of the gentry class, were of modest means, with George's income primarily from farming and supplemented by teaching. Her family valued education, with Jane receiving both tutoring and in-home schooling. She was a voracious reader and had full access to the library and teaching materials her father used to tutor young boys. George encouraged her writing, giving her expensive paper and writing materials. In her teen years, Jane wrote poetry and plays. She was fond of incorporating satire and humor into her writing, likely influenced by her older brother. By age eighteen, she started writing longer works and decided to pursue a career as a writer.

JANE AUSTEN'S CAREER AND LATER LIFE

Much of what we know about Jane's writing career and personal life are from the few surviving letters to her beloved sister, Cassandra. Her first full-length novel, *Elinor and Marianne*, later became *Sense and Sensibility*. Her father attempted to help her get her second novel *First Impressions* (later *Pride and Prejudice*) published by contacting London publishers. Both were heavily revised by Austen before being published, eliminating an epistolary style in favor of third person narration.

The Austen family moved to Bath in 1801, and the following years are a blind spot to scholars as to the day-to-day life of Jane. Many suspect the abrupt move deeply unsettled her life, resulting in a less productive period of writing. Others say she may have had more of a social life in Bath, and therefore less free time to write. Or, she may have been in the process of heavy revisions of previous work.

When *Sense and Sensibility* was finally published in 1811, it was done so anonymously, as was customary for women writers of the time. Though poetry was often published under a woman's name, works of fiction were rarely attributed to women. Her novels were published on commission, meaning the publisher fronted the costs of publication and took a commission of sales. However, the author was responsible for the publication costs should the books not sell. It was of great personal financial risk to accept a publishing deal with these terms, but it ultimately paid off. The books were well-reviewed and many copies were printed. Some even ended up in the hands of the Prince Regent himself.

Jane fell ill in 1816, with what we now believe to be either Addison's disease or Hodgkin's lymphoma. She died in 1817 at age forty-one. When her siblings published her final two novels, *Northanger Abbey* and *Persuasion* after her death, it was the first time they were published under her own name. Her novels were briefly out of print between publishing rights, but have been continuously in print since the 1830s.

ESSENTIAL WORKS OF Jane Austen

Jane Austen's novels are part of the transition away from sensationalist fiction to nineteenth century literary realism. She is credited for her knack for complex dialogue and is one of the first English novelists to use free indirect speech to convey the thoughts of a character. Her ability to use humor and satire to explore the complicated positions of women in society remain relevant today. We consider all her novels to be essential reading.

Sense and Sensibility (1811)

Price and Prejudice (1813)

Mansfield Park (1814)

Emma (1816)

Northanger Abbey (1818)

Persuasion (1818)

RED, WHITE & *Royal* BLUEBERRY

We first started making this cocktail for one of our annual Pride Month bookstore crawls. It was balanced, refreshing, and perfect for hot summer days, so we decided to add it to our regular summer cocktail menu. That being said, it's delicious year-round!

BOOK INSPIRATION

Red, White & Royal Blue by Casey McQuiston (2019). What would happen if the son of the president of the United States fell in love with the prince of England? Your queer fantasy comes true in *Red, White & Royal Blue*. The book kicks off with a not-so-meet-cute altercation between Alex (son of the first female president of the United States) and Prince Henry of England: a highly photographed tumble into a wedding cake. What follows is a slow burn turned steamy romance between two very public men trying to do the most intimate thing in private: fall in love. Readers will love the quippy dialogue, big feelings, and hopeful ending.

1½ ounces (45 ml) vodka

1 ounce (30 ml) chilled blueberry tea

¾ ounce (22 ml) fresh lemon juice

¾ ounce (22 ml) lavender syrup

Soda water, for topping

3 to 5 fresh blueberries, skewered, for garnishing

1. In a shaker filled with ice, combine the vodka, blueberry tea, lemon juice, and lavender syrup.
2. Cover and shake thoroughly until chilled.
3. Strain into a wine glass filled with ice.
4. Top with the soda water.
5. Garnish with the blueberries.

SEX *on the* NORTH BEAR SHORES BEACH

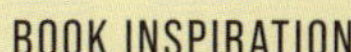

One of the simplest phrases that can drum up the memory of a relaxing vacation is "beach read." The name of the classic cocktail, Sex on the Beach, might induce the memory of the best vacation of your life. So, for Emily Henry's *Beach Read*, we made the obvious connection: Both are designed to be enjoyed during a perfect beach day, and both will make you feel light-hearted and relaxed. The witty repartee between January and Gus makes for a winning combination with a drink that perfectly balances the sour and the sweet.

BOOK INSPIRATION

Beach Read by Emily Henry (2020). January and Gus are old college rivals who reconnect over a summer in the North Bear Shores lake community. Both dealing with writer's block, they challenge themselves to write in each other's genres, swapping romance and literary fiction. As you can imagine—the real romance happens off the page!

6 to 7 fresh raspberries, for muddling

1 ounce (30 ml) vodka

1 ounce (30 ml) peach schnapps

1 ounce (30 ml) triple sec

1 ounce (30 ml) fresh orange juice

1 ounce (30 ml) cranberry juice

Orange slice, for garnishing

1. Place the raspberries in a shaker. Muddle until they are completely broken down and resemble puree. Fill the shaker with ice and add the vodka, peach schnapps, triple sec, orange juice, and cranberry juice.
2. Cover and shake thoroughly until chilled.
3. Double-strain into a highball glass filled with ice.
4. Garnish with the orange slice.

BARTENDER'S MARGIN NOTE

This drink can easily be changed to a mocktail! Simply swap the vodka, peach schnapps, and triple sec for the same quantities of lime juice, lemon juice, and peach nectar.

VIOLET'S ELIXIR

The dramatic universe of *Fourth Wing* is made even more magnificent with this shimmering cocktail in hand. The butterfly pea blossom tea interacts with the lemon juice and changes color from a deep blue to a brilliant purple, transforming itself much like the novel's heroine, Violet. The edible glitter provides a dazzling effect when poured, evoking the magic of the dragons and the world Violet inhabits.

BOOK INSPIRATION

Fourth Wing by Rebecca Yarros (2023). In the first book of the Empyrean series, twenty-year-old Violet Sorrengail begins her story as a fragile Scribe and transforms over time into a powerful leader. After being forced by her mother to attend the Basgiath War College and become a dragon rider, Violet must endure dangerous and grueling competitions against a highly proficient rider, Xaden.

Butterfly Pea Blossom Tea
(makes 8 ounces/240 ml)

¼ cup (approx. 7 grams) butterfly pea flowers

8 ounces (240 ml) boiling water

Cocktail

1 ounce (30 ml) vodka

1 ounce (30 ml) Butterfly Pea Blossom Tea

½ ounce (15 ml) triple sec

½ ounce (15 ml) fresh lemon juice

¼ ounce (7 ml) lavender syrup

Pinch Pixie Dust edible glitter (optional)

Lemon peel, for garnishing

1. **To make the butterfly pea blossom tea:** In a small pot, steep the butterfly pea blossom flowers in the boiling water for 2 minutes. Strain through a fine-mesh strainer into a glass jar or airtight container. Let cool completely. Store in the refrigerator for up to 3 days.
2. **To make the cocktail:** In a shaker filled with ice, combine the vodka, butterfly pea blossom tea, triple sec, lemon juice, lavender syrup, and edible glitter (if using).
3. Cover and shake thoroughly until chilled.
4. Strain into a wine glass filled with ice.
5. Garnish with the lemon peel.

What a Thrill

Whether it's a spine-tingling ghost story, a heart-pounding spy thriller, or a murder mystery that keeps you guessing, this is the type of book that epitomizes the term "page-turner"! While Edgar Allan Poe's short story "The Murders in the Rue Morge" (1841) is credited as the first modern detective story, the origins of horror novels are much older. Many cite Mary Shelley's *Frankenstein* (1818) as among the first, though some would trace the genre's origin to Dante Alighieri's "The Divine Comedy" (~1321).

Classics within these genres are timeless. Bram Stoker's *Dracula* (1897) remains easily readable and has inspired countless adaptations. *The Haunting of Hill House* (1959) by Shirley Jackson is the definitive haunted house story. Agatha Christie set the stage for an entire genre of books and films still being devoured today. Truman Capote went even deeper in *In Cold Blood* (1965) attempting to stare unblinkingly into the eyes of pure human evil and return with something like an explanation.

Contemporary authors utilize aspects of life that we find exhilarating and frightening today. Rumaan Alam's *Leave the World Behind* (2020) fashions a mysterious catastrophe that neuters the technology we depend upon. *Slow Horses* (2010) by Mick Herron flips the slick espionage cliche on its head and instead tells the MI5 story from a group of pariahs solving crime mysteries from the outside looking in.

Whichever your preference, cozying up with a mystery, crime novel, thriller, or horror book works best when accompanied by a delicious cocktail.

MURDER *on the* ORIENT ESPRESSO MARTINI

Our flagship cocktail! Some might say . . . the best espresso martini in New York City. When we added cocktails to our bar, we knew nailing a perfect espresso martini was essential. We source our coffee from local roasters—shout out to two for our local favorites: MUD in Manhattan's East Village and Loveless in Bushwick, Brooklyn—and strongly believe that fresh espresso is truly the key to the flavorful crema that tops the cocktail. If you don't have access to an espresso machine, we highly recommend going to your local coffee shop for some espresso before shaking at home. But in a pinch, you can substitute cold brew or iced coffee. This after-dinner drink will keep you awake just long enough to read a few more pages.

BOOK INSPIRATION

Murder on the Orient Express by Agatha Christie (1934) is a locked-room style story that laid the foundation for how we read mysteries today. The book was inspired by the author's own ride on the Orient Express train to Istanbul!

1 ounce (30 ml) cooled espresso

½ ounce (15 ml) Simple Syrup (page 37)

½ ounce (15 ml) Kahlúa

1½ ounces (45 ml) vodka

3 espresso beans, for garnishing

1. In a shaker filled with ice, combine the espresso, simple syrup, Kahlúa, and vodka.
2. Cover and shake thoroughly until chilled (see Bartender's Margin Note).
3. Strain into a (preferably) chilled martini glass.
4. Garnish with the espresso beans.

BARTENDER'S MARGIN NOTE

A tougher shake of at least 1-minute yields a thick, frothy layer on top known as crema. Ideally, you want the crema to be golden-brown and visible on the glassware for the first ¼ inch (6 mm) of the top of the drink. That makes those first few sips extra creamy and pleasant!

AUTHOR SPOTLIGHT

Agatha Christie

Agatha Christie, born in 1890 in Devon, England, was later dubbed the Queen of Mystery. She was a voracious reader from the age of four, enjoying Dickens and Dumas. Christie was educated in Paris, and later spent time in Egypt with her mother, before returning to England and beginning to write in earnest. In 1914, she married Archibald "Archie" Christie, who was shortly dispatched to serve in the First World War. Christie volunteered with the British Red Cross throughout the war.

Publishing during what is now considered a "Golden Age" of mystery writing, she was rejected six times before finally releasing her first novel, *The Mysterious Affair at Styles,* in 1920. This was the first book featuring her now iconic detective, Hercule Poirot, who appeared in thirty-three novels, plays, and other short stories.

CHRISTIE'S OWN MYSTERY

Agatha Christie herself made headlines when she disappeared for ten days in 1926, following the public dissolution of her marriage. Speculation on her whereabouts was rampant, and even Sherlock Holmes author Sir Arthur Conan Doyle aided the police in the search. She was found checked in to a hospital under the pseudonym of her husband's lover with apparent memory loss. It is unclear what exactly transpired, but doctors believed her to be in a sort of fugue state or nervous breakdown.

Following Christie's convalescence in the Canary Islands, she and her only daughter, Rosalind, returned to England. She officially divorced and set out to travel the world, taking the Orient Express train to Istanbul, and later Iraq, where she met an archeologist who would become her second husband and lifelong partner, Max Mallowan. Mallowan was later knighted

BELOVED AROUND THE WORLD.
Christie is one of the world's most translated authors. Her stage play, *The Mousetrap*, holds the record for longest continuously running play on London's West End, having opened in 1952 and halted only by COVID-19 shutdowns in 2020.

for his work in archaeology, and Christie was promoted to Dame Commander of the Order of the British Empire (DBE). Christie died in 1976 of natural causes. Her estate continues to manage ownership of her works, including film and TV rights, play rights, and portrayals in pop culture.

ESSENTIAL WORKS OF Agatha Christie

Christie was a prolific writer, publishing sixty-six works in her lifetime. She published an additional six novels under the pen name Mary Westmacott. She is considered one of the best-selling authors in history—her book sales are on par with the Bible and Shakespeare. If you don't have time to read her entire oeuvre, here's a good starting point.

The Seven Dials Mystery (1929)

And Then There Were None (1939)

HERCULE POIROT SERIES

The Mysterious Affair at Styles (1921)

The Murder of Roger Ackroyd (1926)

The Mystery of the Blue Train (1928)

Murder on the Orient Express (1934)

Death on the Nile (1937)

Hallowe'en Party (1969)

MISS MARPLE SERIES

The Murder at the Vicarage (1930)

The Body in the Library (1942)

BOOKSELLER'S MARGIN NOTE

While Dr. Frankenstein's creature is often misnamed as Frankenstein itself, the essence of the novel persists. It has been adapted for stage and screen and has inspired countless film adaptions, from Mel Brooks's 1974 horror/comedy Young Frankenstein, *to Yorgos Lanthimos's* Poor Things *in 2023 and Guillermo del Toro's* Frankenstein *in 2025. Dr. Frankenstein's creature endures!*

Dr. Frankenstein's CORPSE REVIVER NO. 2

Our twist on the classic Prohibition-era cocktail, Corpse Reviver No. 2. (Not to be confused with its predecessor No. 1, which is made from cognac, Calvados, and sweet vermouth.) The classic No. 2 typically includes an absinthe rinse, Lillet Blanc, and gin. Intended to be a tart, refreshing drink, the Corpse Reviver family of cocktails are one of the original "hair of the dog" cocktails, meant to perk you up at the beginning of the day! This "Dr. Frankenstein's" edition uses mezcal for an extra smokey punch to the palate. It's slightly herbal, subtly sweet, and powerfully aromatic, ideal for a late afternoon cocktail hour.

BOOK INSPIRATION

Frankenstein by Mary Shelley (1818). Eighteen-year-old Mary Shelley and her social circle spent a rainy summer at a villa in Switzerland competing to come up with the best ghost story. Shelley later said Dr. Frankenstein's monster came to her as a sort of "waking dream," a terrifying vision of a man-made creation of life. She first drafted a short story, originally titled *Frankenstein or The Modern Prometheus*, which was published in 1818 and underwent several revisions. Both the 1818 text and the 1831 version remain in print today. The book received critical success early, and many regard it as one of the first science-fiction stories.

Absinthe spritz (see page 20)

1½ ounces (45 ml) mezcal

¾ ounce (22 ml) grapefruit juice

½ ounce (15 ml) fresh lemon juice

½ ounce (15 ml) Simple Syrup (page 37)

Splash triple sec

Grapefruit wedge, for garnishing

1 star anise pod, for garnishing

1. Spritz a chilled coupe or martini glass with absinthe.
2. In a shaker filled with ice, combine the mezcal, grapefruit juice, lemon juice, simple syrup, and a splash of triple sec.
3. Cover and shake thoroughly until chilled.
4. Strain into the prepared glass.
5. Garnish with the grapefruit wedge and star anise.

BARTENDER'S MARGIN NOTE

Erin is from Wisconsin, and anyone who is from or has visited Wisconsin knows they have a special way of doing Bloodys! The typical Wisconsin Bloody comes with a beer chaser—usually 4 ounces (120 ml) of a local draft pilsner or lager. As for garnishes, there are no plain olives or celery here! Don't be surprised to find any of the following in your Wisconsin-style Bloody Mary: beef jerky, cheese curds, a burger slider, bacon, a slice of bratwurst, or even a whole roast chicken. Feel free to play with garnishes to put your own twist on our Bloody Mary!

In COLD BLOODY MARY

Who doesn't love a classic Bloody Mary? Ordering one in a bar or restaurant can be a gamble—each place has their own recipe, so you never know what you're going to get. It could be extra spicy or have too much or not enough Worcestershire or horseradish. Hopefully, you'll find we've made ours just right, but the beauty of a Bloody Mary is how easy it is to alter the ingredients without entirely changing the composition of the drink, so you can always adjust as you see fit.

BOOK INSPIRATION

In Cold Blood by Truman Capote (1965), considered one of the pioneering true crime works. Capote and author Harper Lee traveled to Kansas to investigate the brutal murder of the Clutter family, which occurred in 1959. In 1960, Capote began compiling extensive notes and interviews with locals, and even the two men on trial for the murder. What followed was a remarkable true crime novel—factual, albeit with embellished scenes of dialogue. The book was not a "whodunit" or even a "why-done-it." Readers already knew the outcome. The story of the victims, the murderers, and the locals was still wildly suspenseful and continues to be compelling to new readers.

2 ounces (60 ml) vodka

4 ounces (120 ml) tomato juice

¼ ounce (7 ml) fresh lemon juice

1½ teaspoons Frank's RedHot Sauce

¾ teaspoon Worcestershire Sauce

½ teaspoon prepared white horseradish

Pinch ground black pepper

2 green olives, for garnishing (optional)

Lemon wedge, for garnishing (optional)

½ celery stalk, for garnishing (optional)

1. In a mixing glass, combine the vodka, tomato juice, lemon juice, hot sauce, Worcestershire Sauce, horseradish, and pepper.
2. Stir thoroughly until flecks of black pepper are distributed evenly throughout.
3. Pour into a highball glass or pint glass filled with ice.
4. Garnish with olives, lemon, or celery (or any combination thereof!).

LEAVE *the* WORLD BEHIND

While we would never suggest drinking to such excess as to literally or figuratively leave the world behind, we do know that a stiff drink at the end of a hard day can help you unwind, ease some tension, and might clear your head. Whether you're heading to a bar to meet friends and catch up, or fixing yourself a drink at home, a strong martini can help leave the world behind, at least temporarily.

BOOK INSPIRATION

Leave the World Behind by Rumaan Alam (2020). A family's getaway is interrupted when the owners of their vacation rental unexpectedly return home, due to a blackout in NYC. Something has happened, but we don't know what. Alam masterfully creates a creeping sense of dread, and the book's release in 2020 served up spine-tingling unease, on top of what we were already experiencing.

Absinthe, for rinsing (see page 20)

2 ounces (60 ml) gin

¾ ounce (22 ml) dry vermouth

Lemon twist, for garnishing

1. Rinse a chilled coupe or martini glass with absinthe.
2. In a mixing glass filled with ice, combine the gin and dry vermouth.
3. Stir thoroughly until chilled.
4. Strain into the prepared glass.
5. Garnish with a lemon twist.

BARTENDER'S MARGIN NOTE

There are infinite types of martinis, but we like to divide them into two categories: classic and modern.

The foundational classic is 2 ounces (60 ml) of gin (or, less traditionally, vodka) with a small amount of dry vermouth and a lemon twist, olive, or onion and is usually stirred, not shaken. Common variations include a Dry Martini (less vermouth), a Dirty Martini (olive brine added), or a Gibson (gin with an onion).

Modern martinis are your Espresso Martinis, Lemon Drops, Chocolate Martinis, etc. These are made with vodka, almost always shaken, and can include virtually anything you can dream up.

The martini may seem haughty and venerable, but there is a type of martini for everybody. Go crazy!

BOOKSELLER'S MARGIN NOTE

Within the broader genre of thriller lies the spy novel, with origins going as far back as the mid to late nineteenth century. Even the fictional detective Sherlock Holmes spied for the British government in a few stories, but it wasn't until the Cold War was in full swing that espionage tales between the major world powers took hold of the popular imagination. Ian Fleming first introduced James Bond in 1953's Casino Royale to great commercial success. But it was John le Carré's focus on the morally gray areas of espionage and the ethical decisions that followed that made Le Carré the king of the spy novel. His influence is widely felt throughout the genre.

SMOKE & MIRRORS

While we're fairly certain Jackson Lamb would never be bothered to make a cocktail (he prefers pulling whisky straight from the bottle he keeps in his desk), we're confident he would enjoy our take on a Rusty Nail. Our version with honey syrup is slightly sweeter, while retaining the smoky Scotch taste and the hint of spice from Drambuie. Lemon and anise give it a subtle aromatic finish. We think it's the perfect fireside sipper.

BOOK INSPIRATION

Herron's *Slough House* series was injected with new life in 2022, thanks to the brilliant TV adaptation starring Gary Oldman as the curmudgeonly Jackson Lamb. The "slow horses" refer to a group of MI5 rejects, trained spies banished to a dumpy office due to their incompetence, or as punishment. Despite their moniker, the group stays relevant as they are roped in to solve the kidnapping case of a British-Pakistani student by a white nationalist group. Herron is carrying on the series, so we will continue to enjoy reading about the mishaps and misadventures of the Slough House misfits.

Honey Syrup

(makes 6 ounces/180 ml)

4 ounces (120 ml) honey

4 ounces (120 ml) hot water

Cocktail

2 ounces (60 ml) Scotch

1 ounce (30 ml) Drambuie liqueur

1 teaspoon Honey Syrup

Lemon slice, for garnishing

1 star anise pod, for garnishing

1. **To make the honey syrup:** In a small pot, combine the honey and water, stirring until dissolved. Let cool completely. Transfer to a glass jar or airtight container. Store in the refrigerator for up to 1 month.
2. **To make the cocktail:** In a mixing glass filled with ice, combine the Scotch, Drambuie, and honey syrup.
3. Stir thoroughly until chilled.
4. Strain into a rocks glass filled with ice.
5. Garnish with the lemon slice and star anise.

Dirty SHIRLEY JACKSON

The Dirty Shirley is an alcoholic version of the classic Shirley Temple drink, believed to have first been concocted in the 1930s in Los Angeles. It has a sweet and innocent base, but the addition of vodka has a "dirty" and corrupting effect.

AUTHOR INSPIRATION
Like this classic drink, the haunting writings of Shirley Jackson often begin with straightforward premises, but eventually the dark psychological depths of the stories are unearthed. Use this drink to give you the liquid courage you need to approach her many chilling gothic classics.

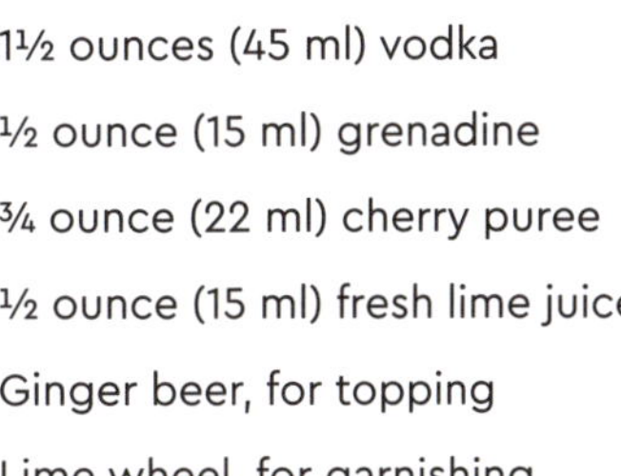

1½ ounces (45 ml) vodka

½ ounce (15 ml) grenadine

¾ ounce (22 ml) cherry puree

½ ounce (15 ml) fresh lime juice

Ginger beer, for topping

Lime wheel, for garnishing

1 to 2 maraschino cherries, skewered, for garnishing

1. In a shaker filled with ice, combine the vodka, grenadine, cherry puree, and lime juice.
2. Cover and shake thoroughly until chilled.
3. Strain into a copper mule mug filled with ice.
4. Top with the ginger beer.
5. Garnish with the lime wheel and skewered maraschino cherry.

AUTHOR SPOTLIGHT

Shirley Jackson

Shirley Jackson's life was short, but her legacy is sure to be everlasting. Raised in a suburb of San Francisco, she attended Syracuse University where she met her future husband and her first story was published in a literary magazine. She attracted nationwide attention in 1948 when she published "The Lottery" in *The New Yorker*. The story's harsh and violent content was met with critical acclaim and public outrage. *The New Yorker* received significant hate mail—an impressive response to a short story. Though it was met with public scrutiny, *The Lottery* became one of the most famous short stories in American literature. Jackson later published two memoirs.

BEYOND THE SHORT STORY

Jackson's next work, her novel *Hangsaman*, focused on a young woman's struggle with mental illness and was based loosely on the disappearance of a college student in Vermont, where she was living at the time. She is perhaps best known for her fifth novel, *The Haunting of Hill House* (1959), which is considered an essential of the horror genre. Stephen King has called this gothic horror story "one of the two great novels of the supernatural in the last hundred years."

Shortly after *The Haunting of Hill House* was published, Jackson's health began to decline, but still, in 1962 she published *We Have Always Lived in the Castle*, a mystery novel that is considered by some to be her greatest work. In 1965, Jackson died at the age of forty-eight of heart failure. In her life she had published six novels and over 200 short stories.

Shirley Jackson's work has inspired and influenced countless artists across the horror and mystery genres, and beyond. Themes of madness, mysticism, and the supernatural are common in her stories, and her writing has captivated audiences for decades.

HAUNTING IN HOLLYWOOD

The Haunting of Hill House was adapted into a film in 1963, titled *The Haunting*. The critically acclaimed film was directed by Academy Award winner, Robert Wise. In 1999, the novel returned to the big screen in a new adaptation starring Liam Neeson and Catherine Zeta Jones.

ESSENTIAL WORKS OF Shirley Jackson

The Lottery is an obvious place to start when reading Shirley Jackson. However, reading Jackson's first and only short story collection to appear in her lifetime, *The Lottery and Other Stories*, will be extremely rewarding. Jackson's original title for this collection was *The Adventures of James Harris*, as characters in several of the stories are named James Harris. Next, we've chosen to list all six of her published novels, each one distinctive, atmospheric, and compelling. Finally are Jackson's two memoirs based on her domestic life as a mother. They are a surprising and humorous departure from her fiction.

SHORT STORIES

The Lottery and Other Stories (1949)

NOVELS

Hangsaman (1951)

The Bird's Nest (1954)

The Sundial (1958)

The Haunting of Hill House (1959)

We Have Always Lived in the Castle (1962)

MEMOIRS

Life Among the Savages (1953)

Raising Demons (1957)

PRACTICALLY *Magical* MARGARITA

A cozy fall cocktail goes hand in hand with something witchy around spooky season, which is why a cocktail based on *Practical Magic* by Alice Hoffman is a no-brainer. Since the book mentions "midnight margaritas," this is also a no-brainer (many likely remember the iconic 1998 film scene in which the sisters and aunts imbibe in pitchers of margaritas at midnight). We love this version of a margarita with an autumnal twist! With apple cider and cinnamon, it's less tart than a traditional margarita, and the sugar and cinnamon rim gives a nice balance of sweetness to the drink. If you want to *truly* replicate the midnight margaritas scene, this would be an easy recipe to multiply by four or six to make pitchers!

BOOK INSPIRATION

Practical Magic by Alice Hoffman (1995). Gillian and Sally Owens are the latest in a long line of powerful witches. Sally marries Michael and hopes to have finally broken the curse that has plagued the women of the family for generations. Devasted upon his death, she yearns to break free of the magical world for the future happiness of her daughters. Gillian shows up after years away with the dead body of her abusive boyfriend in her car, and the sisters return to magic to cover up the incident.

¾ ounce (22 ml) fresh lime juice, plus more for rim (optional)

2 tablespoons granulated sugar, for rim

2 tablespoons ground cinnamon, for rim

1½ ounces (45 ml) tequila

2 ounces (60 ml) apple cider

¾ ounce (22 ml) triple sec

1 cinnamon stick (3 inches/7.5 cm), for garnishing

Apple slice, for garnishing

1. Wet the rim of a rocks glass with water or lime juice.
2. On a small plate, combine the sugar and ground cinnamon and press the rim of the glass down for a partial or full sugar rim.
3. Fill the rocks glass with ice.
4. In a shaker filled with ice, combine the tequila, apple cider, lime juice, and triple sec.
5. Cover and shake thoroughly until chilled.
6. Strain into the prepared glass.
7. Garnish with the cinnamon stick and apple slice.

ROSEMARY'S BABY

Ask any New Yorker and they'll tell you that there is a strange juxtaposition you sometimes feel within the city: surrounded by people and yet surprisingly alone. That eerie contradiction has never been so vividly illustrated as it is in Ira Levin's *Rosemary's Baby*, set in and around the famous and infamous Dakota on the Upper West Side. This cocktail, a riff on a paloma, can be enjoyed alone or among friends. Its tequila heat mixes beautifully with the tangy bitterness from the grapefruit and lime, and the rosemary simple syrup gives it a unique sweetness to tie it all together. If the flavor is too robust and you're feeling the devil inside you coming out, just add more soda water to cut the intensity.

BOOK INSPIRATION

Rosemary's Baby by Ira Levin (1967). Rosemary Woodhouse discovers she is pregnant shortly after having a nightmare involving a sexual encounter with an inhuman creature. She becomes severely ill and is convinced her unborn child is going to be a ritual sacrifice for the occult coven operating within her apartment building, the Bramford. Perhaps best known in its film format, which bears a shockingly loyal-to-the-book interpretation, *Rosemary's Baby* has the uncanny ability to make you feel isolated and disoriented along with its central character in her search for truth in a fun house of suspicion and paranoia.

Rosemary Simple Syrup
(makes 12 ounces/360 ml)

1 cup (200 g) granulated sugar

2 sprigs fresh rosemary

8 ounces (240 ml) boiling water

Cocktail

1½ ounces (45 ml) tequila

1 ounce (30 ml) grapefruit juice

½ ounce (15 ml) fresh lime juice

½ ounce (15 ml) Rosemary Simple Syrup

Soda water, for topping

Fresh rosemary sprig, for garnishing

1. **To make the rosemary simple syrup:** In a small pot, combine the sugar and rosemary. Slowly add the hot water, stirring until the sugar is dissolved. Let steep for 2 hours. Strain through a fine-mesh strainer into a glass jar or airtight container. Let cool completely. Store in the refrigerator for up to 2 weeks.
2. **To make the cocktail:** In a shaker filled with ice, combine the tequila, grapefruit juice, lime juice, and rosemary simple syrup.
3. Cover and shake thoroughly until chilled.
4. Strain into a wine glass filled with ice.
5. Top with the soda water.
6. Garnish with the rosemary sprig.

The THURSDAY MURDER MEZCAL MARGARITA

When Book Club Bar was closed, or in various states of closure, for much of 2020, we noticed a few trends in what people were clamoring to read. One genre that stuck out was mystery. People wanted an escape, and they wanted a cozy mystery and *The Thursday Murder Club* fit the bill perfectly. And this spicy mezcal margarita perfectly fits a fun and spicy murder mystery tale!

BOOK INSPIRATION

The Thursday Murder Club by Richard Osman (2020). Author Richard Osman is experiencing a breakout second career; this is the former TV presenter's debut novel, and the first in his popular murder mystery series. Spunky nursing home residents in England's countryside solve cold cases as a hobby until a crime unfolds around them that only they can solve. His blend of charm, intricately woven mysteries, and character depth have made this series a hit.

¾ ounce (22 ml) fresh lime juice

¾ ounce (22 ml) Simple Syrup (page 37)

2 drops spicy tincture (see Bartender's Margin Notes)

1½ ounces (45 ml) mezcal

Lime wheel or wedge, for garnishing

1. In a shaker filled with ice, combine the lime juice, simple syrup, spicy tincture, and mezcal.
2. Cover and shake thoroughly until chilled.
3. Strain into a rocks glass filled with ice.
4. Garnish with a lime wheel or wedge.

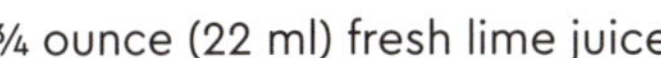

BARTENDER'S MARGIN NOTES

Spicy tinctures can provide an extra kick to give a cocktail some heat, but watch out: Only a few drops are needed to not overwhelm the flavor of the cocktail.

You can buy premade tinctures and test out some flavors, or experiment with batching your own at home: Infuse fresh or dried jalapeños (milder heat), or chili peppers or habanero peppers (stronger heat) in 40 percent ABV vodka or another high-proof neutral spirit in an airtight container for a week or so, to taste (the longer it sits, the stronger the flavor). Be sure to thoroughly wash your hands after handling any peppers.

HEATHCLIFF'S GHOST

Tequila—an earthy, wild spirit (much like Heathcliff's character and the moors themselves)—is central to this paloma-esque cocktail. The citrus in the cocktail is refreshing and bright, while the absinthe rinse and anise have a drifting, perfumed quality without being overpowering. Refreshing—and a little mysterious.

BOOK INSPIRATION
Wuthering Heights by Emily Brontë (1847). While not a thriller in the contemporary sense, Wuthering Heights is often cited amongst the greats of gothic literature, whose traits often include supernatural elements, psychological distress, and an overwhelming sense of place. In this case, the moors of West Yorkshire and the manor of Wuthering Heights serve as the setting for the fraught love turned ghost story of Heathcliff and Catherine.

Absinthe spritz (see page 20)

1½ ounces (45 ml) tequila

¾ ounce (22 ml) grapefruit juice

½ ounce (15 ml) lime juice

½ ounce (15 ml) Simple Syrup (page 37)

Splash triple sec

Grapefruit wedge, for garnishing

1 star anise pod, for garnishing

1. Spritz a wine glass with absinthe, then fill it with ice.
2. In a shaker filled with ice, combine the tequila, grapefruit juice, lime juice, simple syrup, and a splash of triple sec.
3. Cover and shake thoroughly until chilled.
4. Strain into the prepared glass.
5. Top with more ice as needed.
6. Garnish with the grapefruit wedge and star anise.

BOOKSELLER'S MARGIN NOTE

Wuthering Heights *has been adapted in a variety of creative endeavors since its 1847 publication: multiple film adaptations, including a 1920 silent film; a BBC miniseries, opera, ballet production, and radio play production. It continues to be taught in schools, analyzed, and reinterpreted. New readers will find the prose surprisingly contemporary and accessible, while revisits to the text often uncover new interpretations.*

Literary Fiction

Literary fiction is a broad category; the term is typically used to describe literature in contrast to genre fiction (romance, mystery, science-fiction, or fantasy). More character and emotionally driven, novels that fall into this category tend to be the ones more seriously considered by critics or nominated for prestigious awards.

We're focusing on a handful of titles that illustrate the range of literary fiction. Jeffrey Eugenides exploded onto the lit fic scene in 1993 with *The Virgin Suicides* followed by *Middlesex* (2002), which won a Pulitzer. James Baldwin's novels fall squarely into the literary fiction category: immensely interpersonal while exploring larger sociological and political issues.

Ocean Vuong's *On Earth We're Briefly Gorgeous* (2019) is inventive in form, melding an epistolary novel with lyrical prose. *Remarkably Bright Creatures* (2022) by Shelby Van Belt creatively utilizes the perspective of an octopus to explore grief and loneliness. *Tomorrow and Tomorrow and Tomorrow* (2022) by Gabrielle Zevin, follows three friends as they build a video game company, using elements from the games themselves to serve as mirrors to their inner turmoil.

The Nightingale (2015) by Kristin Hannah falls into the subgenre of historical fiction, transporting us to France during WWII. *The Handmaid's Tale* (1985) by Margaret Atwood is a work of speculative fiction, which straddles the line between sci-fi/fantasy and literary fiction. It imagines a future world of patriarchal control, but all plot elements are pulled from our own reality.

Readers in search of a work of fiction that focuses on character development, interpersonal relationships, and general examination of the human condition need look no further than the literary fiction section of their local bookstore!

A VIRGIN SUICIDE Shaker (NA)

Dark, mysterious, and tragic, *The Virgin Suicides* by Jeffrey Eugenides is a novel best approached with a clear head, so we made up a mocktail that tastes delicious but doesn't diminish your senses. This NA drink is a sparkling tropical punch of sorts—lightly tart with a touch of sweetness, and some refreshing bubbles.

BOOK INSPIRATION

The Virgin Suicides by Jeffrey Eugenides (1993). The book opens with the death of the last of the five Lisbon sisters, all of whom have died by suicide. From the perspective of a group of teenage boys who knew the sisters, readers slowly learn the events leading up to the deaths. The novel employs the devastating story of the Lisbon family unraveling to explore the disconnect between placid suburban life and the tumultuous lives of its denizens. Since its publication, this book and the cult classic film it inspired have raised more questions than answers.

1½ ounces (45 ml) pineapple juice

1½ ounces (45 ml) cranberry juice

¾ ounce (22 ml) fresh lime juice

½ ounce (15 ml) grenadine

Soda water, for topping

Pineapple wedge, for garnishing (optional)

1 fresh strawberry, for garnishing (optional)

1. In a shaker filled with ice, combine the pineapple juice, cranberry juice, lime juice, and grenadine.
2. Cover and shake thoroughly until chilled.
3. Strain into a rocks glass filled with ice.
4. Top with the soda water.
5. Garnish with a pineapple wedge or strawberry.

If BOURBON STREET COULD TALK

James Baldwin's *If Beale Street Could Talk* takes place in Harlem but invokes a shared Southern African American history, so we are suggesting a riff on a Sazerac, the legendary New Orleans cocktail. Since Bourbon Street is the most famous New Orleans thoroughfare, we decided to make bourbon our central character, using it to replace the cognac in the original recipe. The Sazerac is a complex cocktail, and the ritual of preparation can mirror the importance of family rituals, which carry important weight in this book. *If Beale Street Could Talk* and the Sazerac, indeed both James Baldwin and the city of New Orleans, are potent symbols of African American history and community.

BOOK INSPIRATION

If Beale Street Could Talk by James Baldwin (1974). A Black love story set in Harlem, we follow Tish and Fonny, a young married couple. After Fonny is accused of rape and is jailed and awaiting trial, Tish learns she is pregnant and must rely on Fonny's family and the broader Harlem community for support.

Absinthe, for rinsing (see page 20)

2 ounces (60 ml) bourbon

¼ ounce (7 ml) Simple Syrup (page 37; see Bartender's Margin Note)

3 to 4 dashes Peychaud's bitters

Dash Angostura bitters (optional, but common)

Lemon peel, for garnishing

1. Rinse a chilled rocks glass with absinthe.
2. In a shaker filled with ice, combine the bourbon, simple syrup, Peychaud's bitters, and Angostura bitters.
3. Cover and shake thoroughly until chilled.
4. Strain into the prepared glass.
5. Garnish with the lemon peel.

BARTENDER'S MARGIN NOTE

To serve this as a more traditional Sazerac, you may muddle 1 sugar cube with the bitters instead of using simple syrup in this recipe. In addition, this drink is traditionally served neat, but you can serve it on ice if desired.

AUTHOR SPOTLIGHT

James Baldwin

James Arthur Jones was born in 1924 to a single mother in Harlem, New York City. He was the grandson of a slave. His mother, Emma Jones, met and married David Baldwin, a Baptist minister, in 1927. James adopted his surname and became older brother to eight siblings from that marriage. He grew up in poverty and described his stepfather as "strict."

Baldwin was an avid reader and interested in writing from young age, and encouraged early on by teachers and mentors: Gertrude E. Ayer, the first Black principal at his elementary school, Countee Cullen, a poet of the Harlem Renaissance and his junior high French teacher, and Bill Porter, a Black Harvard graduate and faculty advisor to his junior high school's newspaper. From age fourteen to seventeen, Baldwin was a preacher at a Pentecostal church, honing his written voice and developing a powerful oratory style.

Baldwin finished high school in 1942. In 1943, his stepfather passed away. To help support his family, he worked various menial day jobs. Eventually, he moved to Greenwich Village and began working as a freelance writer. While there, he met many artists and made connections in the literary community, including Richard Wright, a famous African American novelist who helped Baldwin secure fellowship funding to write his first novel.

WRITER AND ACTIVIST

In 1948, James Baldwin left for Paris, France to escape the racism and homophobia he faced at home in America. There, he struck up friendships with other expats and started several love affairs with young men. His first novel, *Go Tell It on the Mountain* was published in 1953, and an essay collection *Notes of a Native Son* in 1955. The publication of *Giovanni's Room* in 1956 was met with positive reviews, and some controversy over its homoerotic content.

Baldwin returned to the U.S. in 1957 and became active in the civil rights movement. His political activism included public speeches,

THE BALDWIN-BUCKLEY DEBATE

On February 18, 1965, the Cambridge Union Society held a debate between James Baldwin and conservative intellectual, William F. Buckley. Filmed for a live broadcast on the BBC, the two debated the following motion: The American dream is at the expense of the American Negro. He won the debate by a landslide, with 544 votes for his argument, and 164 for Buckley's.

essays, and television appearances, including a now-legendary debate with William F. Buckley. In 1963, *The Fire Next Time*, a work about racial struggle and an urgent appeal for civil rights and equality, was published to much acclaim and landed Baldwin on the cover of *TIME* magazine. He participated in the March on Washington in 1963 and the Selma March in Alabama in 1965. The decades that followed demonstrated Baldwin's emergence as a figure in the burgeoning gay rights movement.

In 1968, to recover from the emotional distress caused by the racial violence he witnessed and the assassinations of his friends Medgar Evers, Malcom X, and Reverend Martin Luther King, Jr., Baldwin returned to France. He settled in St. Paul de Vence, where he continued to write fiction, nonfiction, and poetry. James Baldwin died at his home in 1987.

ESSENTIAL WORKS OF James Baldwin

With eloquence and clarity, James Baldwin tackled issues of race, class, sexuality, and masculinity in America. He is one of the first Black American writers to explore queerness in his work, making him a pioneer for the LGBTQ+ community. In his work and throughout his life, he promoted solidarity and love as the solution to many of society's ugliest problems. His work is beautiful, powerful, and as relevant today as it was in his time. It's hard to pick favorites, but below are some of ours.

NOVELS

Go Tell It on the Mountain (1953)

Giovanni's Room (1956)

Another Country (1962)

Tell Me How Long the Train's Been Gone (1968)

If Beale Street Could Talk (1974)

Just Above My Head (1979)

ESSAY COLLECTIONS

Notes of a Native Son (1955)

The Fire Next Time (1963)

No Name in the Street (1972)

The Devil Finds Work (1976)

The Evidence of Things Not Seen (1985)

NIGHTINGALE NECTAR

Historical fiction is best enjoyed with a classic cocktail, so for *The Nightingale* by Kristin Hannah we are putting our own twist on a Sidecar. Like the sisters in the book, this cocktail originated in France in the early twentieth century. The cocktail was originally named for a soldier who arrived in a motorcycle sidecar, and in our version we have added absinthe, a perennial addition to French drinks and culture. This old cocktail and the chronicles of Vianne and Isabelle are testaments to the timeless themes of the impact of war and the fight for freedom.

BOOK INSPIRATION

The Nightingale by Kristin Hannah (2015). *The Nightingale* explores the ways two sisters, Vianne and Isabelle, cope with the German occupation of France during World War II. Vianne struggles to raise her daughter while her husband is off at war, and endeavors to save the lives of her best friend's Jewish son and others. Isabelle takes an active role in the French Resistance. It takes decades for Vianne to grapple with the enduring effects the war had on their lives.

Absinthe, for rinsing (see page 20)

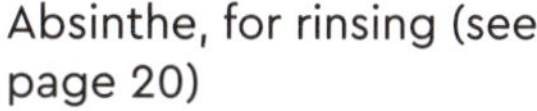

1 tablespoon granulated sugar, for rim (optional)

1½ ounces (45 ml) cognac

¾ ounce (22 ml) fresh lemon juice

½ ounce (15 ml) triple sec

Orange twist, for garnishing

1. Rinse a chilled coupe or martini glass with absinthe.
2. If desired, sugar the rim: Wet the rim of a coupe or martini glass with water. On a small plate, spread the sugar in an even layer and press the rim of the glass down for a partial or full sugar rim.
3. In a shaker filled with ice, combine the cognac, lemon juice, and triple sec.
4. Cover and shake thoroughly until chilled.
5. Strain into the prepared glass.
6. Garnish with the orange twist.

On EARTH *We're* BRIEFLY SOBER(NA)

Ocean Vuong's *On Earth We're Briefly Gorgeous* is lyrical and contemplative, with plenty of clear-headed reflection required. That, coupled with the author's public sobriety, encouraged us to craft an NA cocktail that is refreshing, but not overly sweet, as many mocktails tend to skew.

BOOK INSPIRATION

On Earth We're Briefly Gorgeous by Ocean Vuong (2019). This hybrid work functions as a letter to his illiterate mother, a Vietnamese immigrant raising her son while working in a nail salon. It is part novel, part memoir, quiet, and poetic.

1 ounce (30 ml) fresh lime juice

½ ounce (15 ml) lavender syrup

¼ ounce (7 ml) Honey Syrup (page 81)

Ginger beer, for topping

1 piece rock candy, for garnishing

1. In a shaker filled with ice, combine the lime juice, lavender syrup, and honey syrup.
2. Cover and shake thoroughly until chilled.
3. Strain into a copper mule mug filled with ice.
4. Top with the ginger beer and add more ice, if needed.
5. Garnish with the rock candy.

REMARKABLY *Bright* KRAKEN

Rum drinks and stories of the sea have been linked for as long as molasses has been fermented and distilled, whether it be by Caribbean fishermen, roving pirates, or Papa Hemingway himself. Shelby Van Pelt's *Remarkably Bright Creatures* is a different kind of sea story, told in part by a giant Pacific octopus named Marcellus. For this cocktail, Kraken rum is the obvious choice of a base, and we use pickle brine, cucumber, and sea salt to evoke the brininess of the sea. We recommend pickle brine from our neighbors over at Sweet Pickle Books, a pickle-themed bookstore!

BOOK INSPIRATION

Remarkably Bright Creatures by Shelby Van Pelt (2022). The charming story of the unlikely friendship between Marcellus, an octopus, and Tova, a cleaner at the aquarium where Marcellus lives. It is told partially from the perspective of Marcellus, as he helps Tova process the disappearance of her son years earlier and explores grief, loneliness, and the need for connection.

2 tablespoons coarse sea salt, for rim (optional)

2 ounces (60 ml) Kraken Gold Spiced rum

1 ounce (30 ml) pickle brine

½ ounce (15 ml) Simple Syrup (page 37)

2 dashes hot sauce

Pinch cracked black pepper

3 cucumber slices

Lemon twist, for garnishing

1. If desired, salt the rim: Wet the rim of a rocks glass with water. On a small plate, spread the salt in an even layer and press the rim of the glass down for a partial or full salt rim.
2. In a shaker filled with ice, combine the Kraken Gold Spiced rum, pickle brine, simple syrup, hot sauce, and cracked pepper.
3. Cover and shake thoroughly until chilled.
4. Strain into the prepared glass and stir in the cucumber slices.
5. Garnish with the lemon twist.

The HANDMAID'S COCKTAIL

The Cosmopolitan cocktail, at the height of its *Sex and the City* era popularity, is adapted here to emphasize the color red, the color of the garments worn by the handmaids of Gilead. Both are feminist texts (albeit from wildly different perspectives!). Lightly tart, minimalist, and very drinkable, this is a perfect pre-dinner companion.

BOOK INSPIRATION

The Handmaid's Tale by Margaret Atwood (1985). This dystopian story of a future where women are stripped of their rights has, in the current political climate, felt ominously prophetic. In the novel, we get a first-person narrative from Offred. (We later learn her name is June—Offred refers to Fred, the Gilead Commander to whom she has been assigned.) In this future where the birth rate has sharply dropped, the remaining fertile women are enslaved and forced to procreate. Atwood explores a potential futuristic patriarchal society reminiscent of the Puritanism of the early American settlers.

1¼ ounces (37 ml) vodka

½ ounce (15 ml) cranberry juice

¼ ounce (7 ml) fresh lime juice

¼ ounce (7 ml) triple sec

Lemon twist, for garnishing

1. In a shaker filled with ice, combine the vodka, cranberry juice, lime juice, and triple sec.
2. Cover and shake thoroughly until chilled.
3. Strain into a chilled martini glass.
4. Garnish with the lemon twist.

AUTHOR SPOTLIGHT

Margaret Atwood

Margaret Atwood was born in 1939 in Ottawa, Ontario, Canada. Her father was an entomologist, and she spent much time outdoors, in the rural spaces of Québec and Ontario, where her father frequently traveled for work. While she didn't attend full-time school until the age of twelve, she was a voracious reader and began to write poems and plays as early as six years old. In her teens, she decided she wanted to pursue writing professionally. After graduating from university in Canada, she attended Radcliffe College of Harvard University to pursue a master's degree, graduating in 1961.

A PROLIFIC AND VERSATILE WRITER

Atwood returned to Toronto to teach, and during the 1970s published six volumes of poetry. As her novels began to be published, she gained traction as an influential emerging writer of Canadian literature. *The Handmaid's Tale* was published in 1985; it won the Arthur C. Clarke Award, was a finalist for the Booker Prize, and became one of her most well-known works.

Atwood's breadth of subjects is broad, but she tends to gravitate toward science fiction, or speculative fiction as she prefers to identify it. She emphasizes that all her books could take place within reality on Earth as it is today. While Atwood says her works aren't necessarily feminist texts, many critics analyze the gendered relationships and sexual politics often at the forefront of her novels. She loves to explore different forms of writing, and is a prolific writer: poetry, essays, criticism, stories, graphic novels, children's books, screenplays, and as of 2025, a memoir.

ATWOOD'S CAMEO

In the Hulu series based on her novel, *The Handmaid's Tale*, Atwood not only acted as a co-executive producer on the series but also appeared on screen herself. In a chilling scene in season one, Atwood plays an aunt disciplining Elizabeth Moss's character, Offred, with a slap to the head.

ESSENTIAL WORKS OF Margaret Atwood

Though most known for her famous novels, Atwood's extraordinary talent first came to light through her poetry, with her critically acclaimed collection, *Double Persephone*, in 1961. The rich themes in her poetry set the stage for further exploration in her novels and other works. With over fifty published titles, this list offers a broad range of her work among the many categories in which Atwood is celebrated.

FICTION

The Handmaid's Tale (1985)

Cat's Eye (1988)

Alias Grace (1996)

The Blind Assassin (2000)

Oryx and Crake (2003)

The Penelopiad (2005)

POETRY

Double Persephone (1961)

You Are Happy (1974)

Dearly (2020)

NONFICTION

Writing with Intent: Essays, Reviews, Personal Prose 1983–2005 (2005)

Burning Questions: Essays and Occasional Pieces 2004–2021 (2022)

Book of Lives: A Memoir of Sorts (2025)

SHORT STORIES

Old Babes in the Woods (2023)

TOMORROW, *and* TOMORROW, *and* TEQUILA

Drawing inspiration from a traditional Negroni, we've swapped tequila for gin and added in some sweet and dry vermouth. In this spirit-forward cocktail, you'll taste a bit of bitterness from the Campari, spice from the tequila, and some vegetal aromas from the vermouth. This is an excellent pre-dinner cocktail, or a slow evening sipper!

BOOK INSPIRATION

Tomorrow, and Tomorrow, and Tomorrow by Gabrielle Zevin (2022). It is the magic of literature that a line from a *Macbeth* soliloquy can resonate with audiences centuries later in the title of a novel about video games and friendship. *Tomorrow, and Tomorrow, and Tomorrow* follows decades of friendship between Sadie, Sam, and Marx: as childhood friends, college students, and gaming entrepreneurs. Together, the trio experiences success, chronic illness, and tragedy. Ultimately, the novel explores the work required to maintain lifelong friendships. It's one of the bestselling books we've ever had at Book Club Bar, and we've found that the story resonates with a broad spectrum of readers. There's something in this book for everyone!

1 ounce (30 ml) blanco tequila

1 ounce (30 ml) Campari

½ ounce (15 ml) sweet vermouth

½ ounce (15 ml) dry vermouth

Orange peel, for garnishing

1. In a mixing glass filled with ice, combine the blanco tequila, Campari, sweet vermouth, and dry vermouth.
2. Stir thoroughly until chilled.
3. Strain into a rocks glass filled with ice.
4. Garnish with the orange peel.

Contemporary Classics

Sometimes called "instant classics" or even "future classics," these are books that cement their place in the pantheon of great books the moment they are published. Sometimes it's the critical reception, sometimes the book dominates the cultural zeitgeist, and sometimes it's the book you see everybody reading on the subway, but it's always a book that leaves an eternal impression.

Donna Tartt was an explosive talent right out of college. Her first novel, *The Secret History* (1992), was hailed as a triumph; over thirty years later, we're still in love with it. When *My Brilliant Friend* was published in 2011, the emotional prose immediately struck a chord. The sequels to the story as well as a faithful television adaptation have kept the public's appetite whetted for this rich coming of age story.

John Irving's early works *The World According to Garp* (1978), *The Cider House Rules* (1985), and *A Prayer for Owen Meany* (1989) were celebrated upon publication. Today, it is difficult to imagine the literary world without them. André Aciman's *Call Me by Your Name* (2007) is a powerful story of obsessive romance, and its instantaneous embrace by critics and audiences cemented its legacy. Cormac McCarthy initially wrote *No Country for Old Men* (2005) as a screenplay before turning it into a novel. The film adaptation won four Academy Awards, including Best Picture.

These are some of the modern picks we would consider to be contemporary classics, but there are new ones emerging every year. We are always looking for the next, and when it comes, we'll be happy to find the perfect quaff to match it.

CALL ME *by Your* NECTAR

This peachy (if you know, you know) and lightly tart cocktail will have you dreaming of the Italian countryside in summer. The peach gives a sweet flavor, while the lemon gives it a zesty edge. With the whipped cream signifying a dessert-like indulgence, this drink is perfect for brunch or post-dinner, preferably on a warm summer patio!

BOOK INSPIRATION

Call Me by Your Name by André Aciman (2007). The coming-of-age story tells the love story between the young Elio, who spends his summers with his family in Northern Italy, and Oliver, the slightly older doctoral student who is their houseguest. It perfectly encapsulates the all-consuming first love of youth, in all its embarrassing messiness.

1½ ounces (45 ml) vodka

1½ ounces (45 ml) peach juice or peach nectar

½ ounce (15 ml) fresh lemon juice

Whipped cream, for garnishing

1. In a shaker filled with ice, combine the vodka, peach juice or nectar, and lemon juice.
2. Cover and shake thoroughly until chilled.
3. Strain into a rocks glass filled with ice.
4. Garnish with a big dollop of whipped cream.

BOOKSELLER'S MARGIN NOTES

We are firm believers that reading with your ears still counts as reading! We enjoyed listening to the audiobook version of this title, narrated by Armie Hammer, one of the film's actors. Audiobook performances from narrators, voice actors, or the authors themselves can add a layer of depth to a story. If you haven't explored reading via audiobooks, we encourage you to check out Libro.fm, the purchases from which support independent bookstores.

DONNA *Plum* TARTT

Plum is a rare fruit to find in a cocktail, so when we found this plum liqueur, we knew we had to give it a whirl! This drink is lightly sweet, florally fruity, and refined. The toasted almond bitters provide a subtle nutty aroma, and the Fee Foam gives it a balanced silky texture without being too rich. The cocktail works best as an aperitif or paired with dessert.

AUTHOR INSPIRATION

This cocktail has layers and flavors that reveal themselves over time. Like Donna Tartt herself (elusive, off social media, publishes one novel per decade+, our queen), the Donna Plum Tartt is highly mysterious and refined.

1 ounce (30 ml) vodka

1 ounce (30 ml) Ume plum liqueur

¾ ounce (22 ml) Simple Syrup (page 37)

½ ounce (15 ml) fresh lemon juice

3 to 4 dashes toasted almond bitters

3 to 4 dashes Fee Foam (see Bartender's Margin Note)

Lemon twist, for garnishing

1. In a shaker filled with ice, combine the vodka, plum liqueur, simple syrup, lemon juice, almond bitters, and Fee Foam.
2. Cover and shake thoroughly until chilled.
3. Strain into a chilled martini glass.
4. Garnish with the lemon twist.

BARTENDER'S MARGIN NOTE

Fee Brothers Fee Foam is a vegan alternative to egg whites. It produces a similar creamy, silky texture, without any mess or extra steps. However, you are welcome to swap for egg whites if you prefer!

AUTHOR SPOTLIGHT

Donna Tartt

Donna Tartt was born in Greenwood, Mississippi, in 1963. Coming from a family of avid readers and librarians, she loved reading and began writing from an early age. She wrote her first poem at age five, she had a sonnet published in *Mississippi Review* at age thirteen, and she won awards for essays she wrote in high school. During her freshman year at the University of Mississippi, she was admitted to a graduate course on the short story. The next year, encouraged by her graduate course instructor, she transferred to Bennington College. While a student at Bennington in the 1980s, she penned her first novel—the now widely beloved *The Secret History*—and the ensuing publisher bidding war was unprecedented for a debut novel, instantly solidifying her status in the literary world.

THE WORKS OF DONNA TARTT (SO FAR)

The commercial and critical success of her first novel paved the way for an illustrious career, but Tartt takes very long stretches to complete her contemplative and rich stories. She has only published three books but confirmed in a 2023 interview that she is working on her fourth.

The Secret History (1992)
The original masterclass of dark academia, featuring a tight-knit circle of quasi-friendships, bacchanalia, and murder.

The Little Friend (2002)
The young Harriet, her sister, and parents deal with the aftermath of the unexplained death—presumed to be murder—of the family's nine-year-old son. Set in Tartt's native Mississippi, it is a dark coming of age story. (Also, lots of snakes!)

A LITERARY CLASS

Donna Tartt was not the only influential writer to attend Bennington College in 1986. Her peers included famous writers Bret Easton Ellis and Jonathan Lethem!

The Goldfinch (2013)

Tartt's Pulitzer Prize winning novel follows the young Theodore Decker after he survives a terrorist attack on the Metropolitan Museum of Art that kills his mother, and comes into possession of a prized piece of art.

BOOKSELLER'S MARGIN NOTE

Few authors in recent generations have captured the public imagination quite like Donna Tartt. Her stories are dark and strange, cast with compelling but mystifying people. Whether in a snowstorm in Vermont, a water tower in Mississippi, or a drug den in New York, Tartt's narratives plumb the depths of human darkness and make us ask impossible questions about our own capacity for cruelty.

Outside of her novels, Tartt remains deeply private and has largely eschewed media appearances, building up a mythic persona. Mysterious as she may be to her fans, Tartt has narrated some of her own audiobooks (*The Secret History* and *The Little Friend*), giving readers a chance to connect with her work in a slightly more personal way.

NADER KHALILI

Like WHISKEY *for* CHOCOLATE

Think of this as a more decadent Old Fashioned. Warmly spiced, with the chocolate mole bitters evoking a hint of Mexico, and the orange bitters rounding out the sweetness. Zesty, complex, and warm with a lingering finish—this whiskey drink is an excellent dessert cocktail.

BOOK INSPIRATION

Like Water for Chocolate by Laura Esquivel (1989). Laura Esquivel combines romance, folklore, and magic realism for a tragicomic Mexican story in which food affects people's emotions literally and deeply. Tita, unable to marry her love Pedro due to family tradition, turns her focus instead into cooking. She unintentionally affects those around her when her inner turmoil is transmitted via food. The title is based on the Spanish phrase *como agua para chocolate*, a common idiom meaning that one's emotions are near their boiling point.

1 ounce chocolate syrup, for rim

2 ounces (60 ml) bourbon or rye whiskey

2 dashes orange bitters

2 dashes chocolate mole bitters

Orange peel, for garnishing

1 maraschino cherry, for garnishing

1. On a small plate, drizzle the chocolate syrup onto one side, in an even layer. Press the rim of a rocks glass into it for a partial or full chocolate rim.
2. Fill the rocks glass with ice.
3. In a mixing glass filled with ice, combine the bourbon or whiskey, orange bitters, and chocolate mole bitters.
4. Stir thoroughly until chilled.
5. Strain into the prepared glass.
6. Garnish with the orange peel and cherry.

BARTENDER'S MARGIN NOTE

If you like your drink with extra chocolate, seek out one of the many chocolate-flavored whiskeys on the market. Crown Royal, Ballotin, and 8 Ball produce them, but our favorite is from King's County Distillery.

My BRILLIANT FERRARI

Playing off a more common "Ferrari" shot, we've turned this Fernet and Campari combo into a refreshing spritz to transport you to the Tyrrhenian coastline. While an equal parts Fernet and Campari shot can be intense and bitter, we've added prosecco and orange for a touch of sweetness, to make the drink linger on your palate.

BOOK INSPIRATION

My Brilliant Friend by Elena Ferrante (2011). The first of the esteemed Neapolitan Quartet, *My Brilliant Friend* explores the childhood of Lenu and Lila, as they navigate school, social classes, and the poverty of 1950s working-class Naples. Like its elusive author, the anonymous Elena Ferrante, the friendship of the two women over time is intricate and complex.

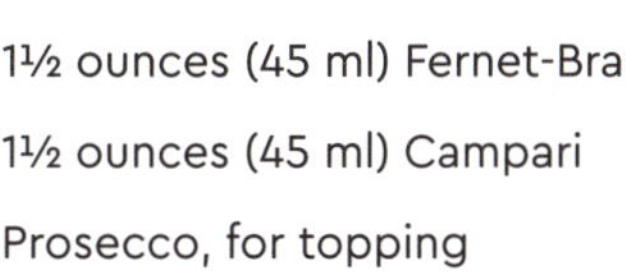

1½ ounces (45 ml) Fernet-Branca

1½ ounces (45 ml) Campari

Prosecco, for topping

Orange peel, for garnishing

1. In a shaker filled with ice, combine the Fernet and Campari.
2. Cover and shake thoroughly until chilled.
3. Strain into a rocks glass filled with ice.
4. Top with the prosecco.
5. Garnish with the orange peel.

NO COUNTRY *for Old-Fashioned* MEN

When choosing a cocktail to pair with *No Country for Old Men* by Cormac McCarthy (2005), we immediately thought of the Old Fashioned. The simplicity and potency of the cocktail matches McCarthy's spare yet powerful storytelling. It is a classic drink with a storied history, yet a simple change (here, maple syrup and cardamom bitters) can completely alter its character. Like an old man looking back on an old world and contemplating the new, it is both bygone and inventive.

BOOK INSPIRATION

No Country for Old Men by Cormac McCarthy (2005). In a Texas town near the Mexico border, Llewelyn Moss stumbles across the aftermath of a drug deal gone wrong: men left dead, another severely injured, and a satchel with millions in cash. Stashing the money, Moss is pursued by the town sheriff, who is eager to save him, and a hired killer named Anton Chigurh.

2 ounces (60 ml) bourbon

¼ ounce (7 ml) maple syrup

2 dashes cardamom bitters

2 dashes Angostura bitters

Orange twist, for garnishing

1. In a mixing glass filled with ice, combine the bourbon, maple syrup, cardamom bitters, and Angostura bitters.
2. Stir thoroughly until chilled.
3. Strain into a rocks glass filled with ice.
4. Garnish with the orange twist.

AUTHOR SPOTLIGHT:

Cormac McCarthy

Cormac McCarthy's legacy is formidable, and he is widely considered to be one of the greatest American authors. Spanning nearly sixty years, his writing career includes twelve novels, two plays, three short stories, and five screenplays. McCarthy was known for being intensely private, avoiding public appearances and interviews throughout his career. His writing, often containing graphic violence and stunning cruelty, is visceral and disarming, and has therefore been adapted into some of Hollywood's most compelling films.

LATE-CAREER SUCCESS

Though his first novel was published in 1965, he first achieved major literary success with *All the Pretty Horses* (1992) which won the National Book Award. Before then, he had been living modestly throughout the United States. *No Country for Old Men* (2005), perhaps his most famous work, was adapted into a film of the same name directed by the Coen brothers starring Tommy Lee Jones, Javier Bardem, and Josh Brolin. The film was showered with praise and won four Academy Awards in 2008 including Best Picture. The following year, he published the post-apocalyptic *The Road* (2006), which won the Pulitzer Prize for Fiction. After *The Road* was chosen as an Oprah's Book Club selection, McCarthy made his first ever television appearance in an interview with Oprah at the Sante Fe Institute where he spoke about the novel and his writing process. His fifth novel, *Blood Meridian* (1985), was not a widespread success when it was first published, but as McCarthy gained renown throughout the literary world, it was revisited by many and is now largely considered to be his greatest work.

McCarthy's writing style is lean and uses very little punctuation, and he is often compared with Ernest Hemingway. This

A FAMOUS TYPEWRITER

In 2009, McCarthy's light blue Olivetti Lettera 32 typewriter, on which he had written several of his novels, sold at Christie's auction house for a shocking $254,500. McCarthy claimed he bought his trusty typewriter decades earlier at a pawnshop for $50. The proceeds were donated to the Sante Fe Institute where he served as a board Trustee for many years.

unadorned style is particularly suited to his storylines, which are often cruel and tragic. Cormac McCarthy's body of work is not for the meek, but it may be the best manifestation of the American soul and character we have. McCarthy passed away from natural causes at 89 years old at his home in Santa Fe, New Mexico.

ESSENTIAL WORKS OF Cormac McCarthy

Cormac McCarthy transported readers to Southern Appalachia, the Texas-Mexico Borderlands, and to a post-apocalyptic America. His first four novels: *The Orchard Keeper* (1965), *Outer Dark* (1968), *Child of God* (1973), and *Suttree* (1979) sold modestly, making McCarthy relatively unknown. It wasn't until the publication of *All the Pretty Horses* did McCarthy achieve fame and commercial success. Below is a list of what are arguably his most famous works.

Suttree (1978)

Blood Meridian (1985)

No Country for Old Men (2005)

The Road (2006)

THE BORDER TRILOGY

All the Pretty Horses (1992)

The Crossing (1994)

Cities of the Plain (1998)

THE PASSENGER SERIES

The Passenger (2022)

Stella Maris (2022)

The CIDER HOUSE MULES

We wanted this cocktail to reflect the Worthington family apple orchard estate so frequently referenced in the book. Our twist on a Moscow Mule contains a cinnamon simple syrup as well as apple cider. It's a refreshing drink that contains the pleasant New England fall vibe so often referenced in Irving novels.

BOOK INSPIRATION

Upon publication, *The Cider House Rules* quickly became one of John Irving's standout novels. Set in post-WWII rural Maine, the bildungsroman focuses on Homer Wells, growing up in an orphanage called St. Cloud's under the care of Dr. Wilbur Larch, an obstetrician who performs abortions for women requiring his care. There is a wide cast of memorable characters, with strong personalities and viewpoints, and so much to unpack with this novel: class inequities, a women's right to healthcare, and moral obligations to family and community. We highly recommend this one as a book club pick, and if you enjoyed it, Irving's *Queen Esther* (2025), while not technically a sequel, returns to the world of St. Cloud's.

Cinnamon Simple Syrup

(makes 12 ounces/360 ml)

1 cup (200 g) granulated sugar

2 to 3 cinnamon sticks (3 inches/7.5 cm each)

8 ounces (240 ml) boiling water

Cocktail

1½ ounces (45 ml) rum

½ ounce (15 ml) Cinnamon Simple Syrup

½ ounce (15 ml) apple cider

Ginger beer, for topping

Apple slice, for garnishing

1 cinnamon stick (3 inches/7.5 cm), for garnishing

1. **To make the cinnamon simple syrup:** In a small pot, combine the sugar and cinnamon sticks. Slowly add the hot water, stirring until the sugar is dissolved. Let cool completely. Strain through a fine-mesh strainer into a glass jar or airtight container. Store in the refrigerator for up to 2 weeks.
2. **To make the cocktail:** In a shaker filled with ice, combine the rum, cinnamon simple syrup, and apple cider.
3. Cover and shake thoroughly until chilled.
4. Strain into a copper mule mug filled with ice.
5. Top with the ginger beer.
6. Garnish with the apple slice and cinnamon stick.

The PINEAPPLE RUM DIARY

This riff on a daiquiri is a tropical cooler that is rum-forward, with tart lime being mellowed out by soothing pineapple juice, and the warm spice of cinnamon in the background. It's perfect to sip on while you page through any story set in a strange, tropical land, and you might find yourself closer to the narrative than you thought.

BOOK INSPIRATION

The Rum Diary by Hunter S. Thompson (1998). Hunter S. Thompson is well known, perhaps equally, for his biting wit and his penchant for debauchery. *Fear and Loathing in Las Vegas* (1971) had already been made into an influential motion picture by the time *The Rum Diary* was even discovered (by Johnny Depp, of all people) in 1998, though it was penned almost forty years earlier. Like *Fear and Loathing*, it is a blurry travelogue filled with sharp insight and questionable decisions. Typical of Thompson's gonzo journalistic style, the narrator is often difficult to separate from the author himself.

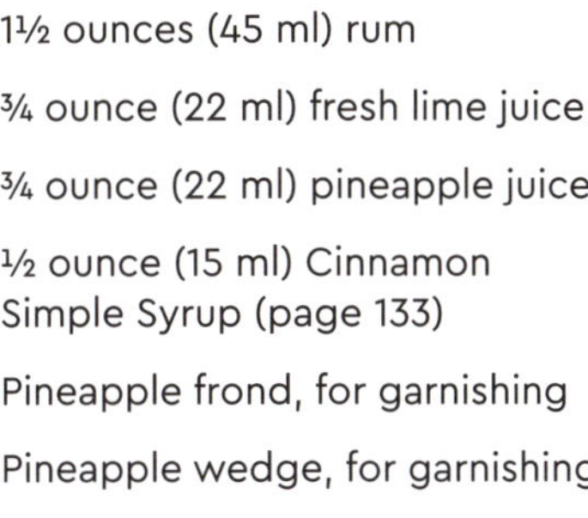

1½ ounces (45 ml) rum

¾ ounce (22 ml) fresh lime juice

¾ ounce (22 ml) pineapple juice

½ ounce (15 ml) Cinnamon Simple Syrup (page 133)

Pineapple frond, for garnishing

Pineapple wedge, for garnishing

1. In a shaker filled with ice, combine the rum, lime juice, pineapple juice, and cinnamon simple syrup.
2. Cover and shake thoroughly until chilled.
3. Strain into a rocks glass filled with ice.
4. Garnish with the pineapple frond and wedge.

Timeless Classics

Historically, classics have been Euro-American centric, skewing white and male, and often exclusionary of large swaths of the population. The definition of a classic is certainly more open to interpretation today and continues to be evaluated as tastes change and time passes. That said, those considered classics tend to be works with evergreen themes and universal struggles that remain relevant long after publication.

Zora Neale Hurston's *Their Eyes Were Watching God* (1937) is a classic of Harlem Renaissance literature, a movement that upended racist stereotypes and ushered in a new era of Black storytelling. Simone de Beauvoir and Betty Friedan are two writers and thinkers who paved the way for feminist expression and thought. Hemingway's universal themes of perseverance, friendship, and a search for meaning explored in *The Sun Also Rises* (1926) and *The Old Man and the Sea* (1952) continue to be pertinent.

In John Steinbeck's *The Grapes of Wrath* (1939), the characters struggle with a quest for dignity, balancing individual versus communal needs, and economic injustice.

Themes of mental health, particularly abuse of power, conformity, and superficiality, are explored in Gustave Flaubert's *Madame Bovary* (1856), Ken Kesey's *One Flew Over the Cuckoo's Nest* (1962), and Oscar Wilde's *The Picture of Dorian Grey* (1890). Edith Wharton's explorations of the Gilded Age, as exemplified in *The Age of Innocence* (1920), continue to be relevant as income inequality is at the forefront of political conversation today.

The works of literature to be added to the classics canon is a question for future generations, but we expect the themes listed above to continue to be repeated in new and interesting ways that resonate with the audiences of today and of the future.

The DELUGE

We are big fans of the humble gimlet—a classic cocktail made of gin, lime juice, and sugar, initially created to fight scurvy. The lime perfectly balances the gin for a simple yet delicious libation. Inspired by Zora Neale Hurston's *Their Eyes Were Watching God* (1937), this version incorporates blue curaçao for a touch of sweetness and, more importantly, to create a beautiful blue presentation. Representing the hurricane and ensuing flood that overtakes the Everglades, this drink's power is a symbol of nature's might and majesty, and humanity's struggle to tame it.

BOOK INSPIRATION

Their Eyes Were Watching God by Zora Neale Hurston (1937). This novel follows generations of women in the early post-slavery era of the Florida Everglades. Janie is recounting her life story, starting with her grandmother Nanny's rape by her white enslaver and ensuing pregnancy with Leafy, Janie's mother. Janie's story hits a turning point during the 1928 Okeechobee hurricane, one of the deadliest in U.S. history, and the traumatic events that follow.

1 ounce (30 ml) gin

1 ounce (30 ml) blue curaçao

1 ounce (30 ml) fresh lime juice

Lime wheel, for garnishing

1. In a shaker filled with ice, combine the gin, blue curacao, and lime juice.
2. Cover and shake thoroughly until chilled.
3. Strain into a chilled martini glass or coupe.
4. Garnish with the lime wheel.

THE FRIENDSHIP POEMS OF RUMI
THE LOVE POEMS OF RUMI
SIDDHARTHA

DE BEAUVOIR *75*

This cocktail is inspired by the traditional French 75 (gin, lemon juice, simple syrup, and a dry sparkling white wine). We've created a slightly more complex French 75 using an Earl Grey tea–based simple syrup. As a bookstore with a cafe and full cocktail bar, we enjoy combining spirits with a caffeinated beverage. This one isn't as caffeine-forward as an espresso martini but has a bit of a kick compared to a traditional French 75.

AUTHOR INSPIRATION

We maintain that Simone de Beauvoir, a lifelong tea-drinker known to frequent iconic Parisian cafes such as Les Deux Magots, would have enjoyed combining tea with gin in our version of the French 75. Widely thought to have originated in Paris at the end of the first World War, this is a drink that certainly would have been shaken in the bars and literary salons of Paris during de Beauvoir's lifetime!

Earl Grey Simple Syrup

(makes 12 ounces/360 ml)

1 cup (200 g) granulated sugar

2 ounces loose leaf Earl Grey tea

8 ounces (240 ml) boiling water

Cocktail

1 ounce (30 ml) gin

½ ounce (15 ml) fresh lemon juice

½ ounce (15 ml) Earl Grey Simple Syrup

Prosecco, for topping

Lemon twist, for garnishing

1. **To make the Earl Grey simple syrup:** In a small pot, combine the sugar and tea. Slowly add the hot water, stirring until the sugar is dissolved. Let steep for 1 hour. Strain through a fine-mesh strainer into a glass jar or airtight container. Let cool completely. Store in the refrigerator for up to 2 weeks.
2. **To make the cocktail:** In a shaker filled with ice, combine the gin, lemon juice, and Earl Grey simple syrup.
3. Cover and shake thoroughly until chilled.
4. Strain into a flute or coupe glass.
5. Top with the prosecco.
6. Garnish with the lemon twist.

AUTHOR SPOTLIGHT

Simone de Beauvoir

Simone de Beauvoir was born into a bourgeois Parisian family in 1908. Her father, an aspiring actor turned lawyer, was instrumental in encouraging her education. De Beauvoir was enrolled in prestigious schools with rigorous coursework. After her family lost much of their money in the years following World War I, and the dowry that would have been Simone's was depleted, she knew she would have to rely on herself, and her education, to forge her own path in the world.

During her undergraduate and later postgraduate work, she was a student of mathematics, literature, and philosophy. At the Sorbonne, she was one of the few early women to be awarded a diploma in philosophy. Among her classmates were Jean-Paul Sartre, Simone Weil, Paul Nizan, and René Maheu. The group highly influenced each other and propelled each other's work within the French existentialist movement.

PUSHING FEMINISM FORWARD

Throughout the course of her career, De Beauvoir wrote novels, essays, and feminist and existentialist philosophical texts. *The Second Sex*, published in 1949, is her most well-known and influential work. In it, she argues that "one is not born but becomes a woman," one of the first articulated distinctions between biological sex and gender, and possibly the most famous line of feminist text ever written.

The work maintains that the "otherness" or mystery of women has allowed men to establish and rule a patriarchal society. Women ought to be able to make choices for themselves, to transcend the positions where they were previously relegated, to choose their own freedom. Later feminist leaders, such as Betty Friedan, credit De Beauvoir's *The Second Sex* as the launch pad for the second wave feminist movement.

De Beauvoir was an outspoken critic of the institution of marriage, arguing it was dangerous for men to be saddled with the financial responsibility of a family, and to women who were dependent on men for their survival. True to her convictions, she never married, but she was in a longtime partnership with Jean-Paul Sartre until his death in 1980. They were together for fifty-one years and had no children.

De Beauvoir passed away in Paris in 1986. Her legacy as a multifaceted writer, existentialist thinker, and feminist activist endures.

ESSENTIAL WORKS OF
Simone de Beauvoir

Simone de Beauvoir's *The Second Sex* was a groundbreaking text for feminist discourse and is still relevant today. It's her best-known work, for good reason, but some might find it an intimidating starting point. Luckily, she published so much more than that and she had a broad range. With novels, essays, short stories, memoirs, and biographies, there are many ways to enter her intellectual world. For a well-rounded and comprehensive dive into her work, these are the books we recommend.

NONFICTION AND PHILOSOPHICAL WORKS

The Ethics of Ambiguity (1947)

America Day by Day (1948)

The Second Sex (1949)

Memoirs of a Dutiful Daughter (1958)

The Coming of Age (1970)

Adieux: A Farewell to Sartre (1981)

NOVELS

She Came to Stay (1943)

The Blood of Others (1945)

The Mandarins (1954)

The Woman Destroyed (1967)

FEMININE *Mezcal* MYSTIQUE

This cocktail is complex: The creamy, tart lemon noticed upon first taste gives way to an underlying smoky mezcal bite. We've used maple and cardamom to balance out the earthy mezcal for a crisp, autumnal drink.

BOOK INSPIRATION

The Feminine Mystique by Betty Friedan (1963). Widely credited with kicking off second-wave feminism, *The Feminine Mystique* is one of the most influential nonfiction books of the twentieth century. What began as a survey of Friedan's former Smith College classmates turned into a larger exploration of the discontent and unfulfillment that many suburban housewives were experiencing in the 1950s and '60s.

1½ ounces (45 ml) mezcal

¾ ounce (22 ml) fresh lemon juice

¾ ounce (22 ml) maple syrup

2 dashes cardamom bitters

4 dashes Fee Foam (see page 121)

Lemon twist, for garnishing

1. In a shaker filled with ice, combine the mezcal, lemon juice, maple syrup, cardamom bitters, and Fee Foam.
2. Cover and shake thoroughly until chilled.
3. Strain into a rocks glass filled with ice.
4. Garnish with the lemon twist.

GRAPEFRUITS *of* WRATH

Sometimes our drinks are closely inspired by the content of a book, and other times we stumble on a cute play on words and work backwards. This one falls into the latter category; after all, what can we say about the American Dust Bowl that wasn't already written in John Steinbeck's brilliant epic *The Grapes of Wrath*? This is our take on a Paloma, and the mint really enhances the flavor profile of the classic drink. The aroma hits right when you lift the glass, so breathe it in and take a long sip.

BOOK INSPIRATION

The Grapes of Wrath by John Steinbeck (1939). Set during the Great Depression, Steinbeck's iconic novel tells the story of the Joad family. Due to immense economic hardship, primarily caused by agricultural industry changes, they are driven from their home in Oklahoma and seek respite further west, heading to California.

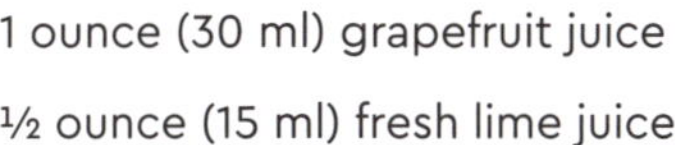

1 ounce (30 ml) grapefruit juice

½ ounce (15 ml) fresh lime juice

½ ounce (15 ml) Mint Simple Syrup (page 35)

1½ (45 ml) ounces tequila

Soda water, for topping

Fresh mint, for garnishing (optional)

Grapefruit half-wheel, for garnishing (optional)

1. In a shaker filled with ice, combine the grapefruit juice, lime juice, mint simple syrup, and tequila.
2. Cover and shake thoroughly until chilled.
3. Strain into a rocks glass filled with ice.
4. Top with the soda water.
5. Garnish with fresh mint, first smacking the leaves in your palm to release their scent, or a grapefruit half-wheel.

AUTHOR SPOTLIGHT

John Steinbeck

John Steinbeck is one of the most celebrated writers in American history, and his titles are some of the most widely read novels today. While other writers of his generation can, at times, feel antiquated, Steinbeck's prose is timeless, and his messages remain significant and meaningful in the present day.

A VOICE FOR THE PEOPLE

From the beginning, Steinbeck was a fervent voice for working people. Throughout his career, he highlighted characters from the lower classes, humanizing the working poor in the eyes of millions of readers. *In Glorious Battle* tells the story of laborers organizing for fair wages and working conditions. *Of Mice and Men* is an intimate narrative about migrant workers trying to survive during the Great Depression. Before writing *The Grapes of Wrath*, Steinbeck visited the slums in California's Central Valley and was moved to craft a story based on the struggles of migrant agricultural workers.

While the Great Depression in all its gravity served as the backdrop for these extraordinary works of literature, the humanity of the characters and the empathy they elicit is the ultimate triumph of all three. Steinbeck was met with scathing backlash due to his perceived fondness for Communism. *The Grapes of Wrath* was banned in several public schools and libraries, and he received threats over the text. "The vilification of me out here from the large landowners and bankers is pretty bad," Steinbeck wrote.

The apotheosis of his career was his magnum opus *East of Eden*, which combined biblical stories with his own family history. He considered it to be the culmination of his career's work, and the sum of everything he

A MASTERPIECE IN LONGHAND

Steinbeck wrote the original manuscript of *The Grapes of Wrath* by hand in long ledgers. His wife, Carole Steinbeck, would then proofread and type up the pages. In 2021, SP Books published the original hand-written manuscript in a limited-edition package, giving readers a close look at Steinbeck's work and process.

learned as a writer. Set in Salinas Valley, California, Steinbeck's childhood hometown, it explores the perennial themes of sibling rivalry, good versus evil, and free will versus fate.

Above all, his body of work stands as a testament to human compassion because he channels an extraordinary ability to put the reader in the position of his characters through his rich storytelling.

ESSENTIAL WORKS OF John Steinbeck

John Steinbeck's collection of works is vast, with seventeen novels and six works of nonfiction in addition to his short stories and screenplays. Along with commercial success, the following titles enjoyed great critical acclaim, including The Pulitzer Prize and The National Book Award for *The Grapes of Wrath* in 1940.

Tortilla Flat (1935)

In Dubious Battle (1936)

Of Mice and Men (1937)

The Grapes of Wrath (1939)

Cannery Row (1945)

The Pearl (1947)

East of Eden (1952)

Travels with Charley: In Search of America (1962)

Madame BOULEVARDIER

As a cocktail bar with a functioning café, we find that our customers are often asking for drinks that have a little pick-me-up. For our take on a boulevardier, the classic spirit-forward whiskey and Campari combo, we wanted to infuse some caffeine to make it special. Like Flaubert's masterpiece *Madame Bovary* (1856), the boulevardier also has French origins and is celebrated the world over. This one has a nice dose of whiskey and Campari to take the edge off, and the coffee infusion to bring the edge back.

BOOK INSPIRATION

Madame Bovary by Gustave Flaubert (1856). Emma Bovary, the second wife of a kind country doctor, becomes bored and dissatisfied with her life. She embarks on multiple romantic affairs as well as lavish spending, both of which lead her to despair. Flaubert expertly tackles issues of societal expectations and gender roles, and the novel is widely considered to be ahead of its time.

Coffee-Infused Campari

½ ounce (14 g) ground coffee

8½ ounces (255 ml) Campari

Cocktail

1 ounce (30 ml) whiskey

1 ounce (30 ml) Coffee-Infused Campari

1 ounce (30 ml) sweet vermouth

2 dashes Aztec chocolate bitters

Orange twist, for garnishing

1. **To make the coffee-infused Campari:** Scoop the coffee into a regular coffee filter and tie it closed with kitchen twine. Place it in a glass jar with a lid and top it with the Campari. Let steep for 24 hours. Remove the coffee filter, making sure to squeeze out all the liquid. Store the jar in the refrigerator for up to 1 month.
2. **To make the cocktail:** In a mixing glass filled with ice, combine the whiskey, coffee-infused Campari, vermouth, and chocolate bitters.
3. Stir thoroughly until chilled.
4. Strain into a rocks glass filled with ice.
5. Garnish with the orange twist.

OLD FASHIONED MAN *and the* SEA

Hemingway's novels are especially suited to cocktail pairings: There are two in this book (see The Tequila Sun Also Rises on page 163). It is fitting, as Hemingway was a world-famous drinker. Like his writing, his favorite drinks were straightforward and uncomplicated, so we put our own twist on a classic cocktail. The Old Fashioned first appeared in the early nineteenth century and was so named because cocktails were becoming more complex and flashier. This is a spirit-forward cocktail (just like Papa would have liked) so pick a quality bourbon and get peachy!

BOOK INSPIRATION

The Old Man and the Sea by Ernest Hemingway (1952). Thematically related to *Moby-Dick* (1851) by Herman Melville, *The Old Man and the Sea* is a classic tale of man versus nature. Santiago, an experienced fisherman, and his protégé Manolin break a dry spell of fishing by hooking the largest marlin they've ever encountered. What ensues is a battle of wills between the man and fish, and deep kinship and respect.

2 ounces (60 ml) bourbon

¼ ounce (7 ml) peach syrup

2 dashes peach bitters

2 dashes Angostura bitters

Orange twist, for garnishing

1. In a mixing glass filled with ice, combine the bourbon, peach syrup, peach bitters, and Angostura bitters.
2. Stir thoroughly until chilled.
3. Strain into a rocks glass filled with ice.
4. Garnish with the orange twist.

One FLEW *Over the* CUCUMBER'S NEST

One Flew Over the Cuckoo's Nest can be a little heavy, so here is a tasty drink to accompany your contemplation. You'll enjoy the earthy tequila backbone of this cocktail, balanced by refreshing cucumber and zesty lime, with a touch of spicy bitters. Its garden party-meets-cocktail hour vibe is bright and revitalizing.

BOOK INSPIRATION

One Flew Over the Cuckoo's Nest by Ken Kesey (1962). This novel is best known for the transcendent film adaptation, but the book examines the neurodivergent mind with a depth that only text can employ. Widely banned for its graphic scenes involving sex and violence, the core of the narrative is about empathy and individuality. It was released in the midst of the Civil Rights Movement, and Americans were beginning to rethink institutionalization; as we continue to ask these difficult questions, this book is as relevant as ever.

Marinated Cucumber

1 medium Kirby cucumber, thinly sliced

3 tablespoons sesame oil

1 piece (1 inch/2.5 cm) fresh ginger, grated

Pinch table salt

Cocktail

1½ ounces (45 ml) tequila

¾ ounce (22 ml) fresh lime juice

½ ounce (15 ml) Simple Syrup (page 37)

3 Marinated Cucumber slices

½ ounce (15 ml) cucumber marinade

1 to 2 dashes habanero bitters

1 cucumber ribbon, skewered, for garnishing

1. **To make the marinated cucumber:** In a small bowl, combine the cucumber slices, sesame oil, grated ginger, and a hearty pinch of salt. Let marinate for 20 minutes, then strain the marinade through a fine-mesh strainer into a glass jar or airtight container, reserving the cucumber slices. Store any remaining marinade in the refrigerator for up to 3 days.

2. **To make the cocktail:** In a shaker filled with ice, combine the tequila, lime juice, simple syrup, cucumber slices, cucumber marinade, and bitters.

3. Cover and shake thoroughly until chilled.

4. Strain into a rocks glass filled with ice.

5. Garnish with the skewered cucumber ribbon.

The PICTURE *of* DORIAN EARL GREY

We sometimes call Book Club Bar "a bookstore for sinners," because we're open late, we serve strong drinks, and we're located in neighborhoods best known for nightlife. We like to think Oscar Wilde, a famous imbiber, would have liked the concept and this cocktail. Be warned: This may at first seem like a sweetened tea drink, but gin is a powerful spirit.

BOOK INSPIRATION

The Picture of Dorian Gray by Oscar Wilde (1890). Dorian Gray impulsively sells his soul to acquire a portrait of himself that ages, while he stays eternally young. He begins his story as a naif but eventually his passion to experience everything in life leads him to the dark side of hedonism. His supernatural portrait keeps his consequences at bay.

1½ ounces (45 ml) gin

1½ ounces (45 ml) Earl Grey Simple Syrup (page 141)

¾ ounce (22 ml) fresh lemon juice

½ ounce (15 ml) vanilla syrup

Orange wheel, for garnishing

1. In a shaker filled with ice, combine the gin, Earl Grey simple syrup, lemon juice, and vanilla syrup.
2. Cover and shake thoroughly until chilled.
3. Strain into a rocks glass filled with ice.
4. Garnish with the orange wheel.

The SAGE *of* INNOCENCE

Edith Wharton's *The Age of Innocence* is a classic novel set in New York's Gilded Age. For this cocktail, we wanted to employ a modern twist on a classic, simple drink. The Old Fashioned is itself a relic of the Gilded Age, and like the characters of the novel, it is refined and timeless. The sage simple syrup and garnish introduce a potent taste and aroma to an otherwise familiar drink. Timeless classics always leave a new impression when experienced through a modern lens.

BOOK INSPIRATION

The Age of Innocence by Edith Wharton (1920). An upper-class couple, Newland Archer and May Welland, are about to be married. Theirs is an arrangement based on the status of their families rather than their affection for each other. When Newland meets May's fascinating cousin, Ellen, he instantly becomes infatuated and questions his future with May. Wharton expertly examines the struggle between societal expectations and an individual's own desire.

Sage Brown Sugar Simple Syrup
(makes 12 ounces/360 ml)

1 cup (150 g) loosely packed dark brown sugar

8 sage leaves, stems removed

Pinch table salt

1 cup (240 ml) water

Cocktail

2 ounces (60 ml) rye whiskey

½ ounce (15 ml) Sage Brown Sugar Simple Syrup

2 dashes Angostura bitters

2 dashes orange bitters

Sage leaf, for garnishing

1. **To make the sage brown sugar simple syrup:** In a small pot, combine the brown sugar, sage leaves, salt, and water; heat over medium heat, stirring until the sugar is dissolved. Reduce the heat to low and let simmer for 1 minute. Remove from the heat and let cool completely, about 30 minutes. Strain through a fine-mesh strainer into a glass jar or airtight container. Store in the refrigerator for up to 2 weeks.
2. **To make the cocktail:** In a shaker filled with ice, combine the rye, sage brown sugar simple syrup, Angostura bitters, and orange bitters.
3. Cover and shake thoroughly until chilled.
4. Strain into a rocks glass filled with ice.
5. Garnish with the sage leaf, first smacking the leaf in your palm to release its scent.

AUTHOR SPOTLIGHT

Edith Wharton

Edith Newbold Jones was born to a distinguished upper-class family in New York City in 1862. Her paternal family, the Joneses, came from real estate wealth. She was related to the Rensselaers, a prestigious Dutch patroon family. Educated by talented governesses and tutors at home and in Europe, where the family lived for six years, she was fluent in French, German, and Italian, and read voraciously. She also wrote short stories and poetry. At age sixteen, *Verses*, a book of her poems, was privately published. While her father used his connections to get her published, her mother disapproved of her writing and discouraged the endeavor. Born into a society with strict rules and a time when securing a proper marriage was considered the greatest achievement for a woman, Edith went on to shatter societal expectations and norms, becoming the first woman to receive the Pulitzer Prize.

FROM DEBUTANTE TO HONORARY DOCTORATE

Edith Jones made her debut in society in 1879, at age seventeen, and eventually married Edward Wharton, a wealthy Boston banker, in 1885. Initially, the couple lived between New York City, on Park Avenue and Newport, Rhode Island, with frequent visits to Europe. Edith was incredibly involved in the remodeling of their Newport home, Land's End, and co-authored *The Decoration of Houses* (1897), a book on design and architecture, with Ogden Codman, Jr. Two short story collections followed: *The Greater Inclination* (1899) and *Crucial Instances* (1901).

In 1901, the Whartons bought land in Lenox, Massachusetts. The Mount, their Lenox estate, was designed by Edith and built in 1902. There, she wrote some of her greatest works, including her first novel, *The Valley of Decision* (1902), *The House of Mirth* (1905), and *Ethan Frome* (1911). As she was achieving professional success, Edward Wharton's mental stability was deteriorating, along with their marriage. The couple sold The Mount in 1911 and divorced in 1913.

Edith Wharton moved to Paris in 1913. When World War I broke out in 1914, she organized several charitable and humanitarian relief efforts, including schools and hostels for refugees, and convalescent homes for tuberculosis patients. She also witnessed and reported on the war from the front lines. *Fighting France: From Dunkerque to Belfort* (1918) is a collection of her 1915 reporting for *Scribner's Magazine*. In 1916, Wharton received the French Legion of Honour.

At the end of the war, Wharton moved out of Paris to the village of St. Brice-sous-Forêt. In 1920 she acquired a chateau in the south of France. In 1921, her novel, *The Age of Innocence*

(1920), won the Pulitzer Prize for fiction. She split her time between her two homes and continued to write prolifically, travel, and garden. After moving to France, she only returned to the United States two times. Her final visit was in 1923, to receive an Honorary Doctorate from Yale. She died in 1937, age 75.

ESSENTIAL WORKS OF Edith Wharton

Wharton didn't publish her first novel until she was forty, but she was incredibly productive and published over fifty books. Her novels, reflecting her privileged upbringing, are often cited as examples of peak Gilded Age storytelling. She used dramatic irony to critique the mores of the period. In addition, she wrote plays, short stories, criticism, war reports, and a memoir, as well as books on architecture, interior design, gardens, and travel. There's so much to choose from, but we're particularly fond of her fiction. Below are our must-reads.

The House of Mirth (1905)

Ethan Frome (1911)

The Custom of the Country (1913)

The Age of Innocence (1920)

Twilight Sleep (1927)

The Buccaneers (1938)

The New York Stories of Edith Wharton (2007)

The TEQUILA SUN *Also* RISES

Our take on the vibrant tequila sunrise cocktail mirrors the Spanish fiesta of *The Sun Also Rises*. Like the Pamplona festival, this cocktail is summery and refreshing. Be sure to slowly layer in the grenadine for true sunrise effect!

BOOK INSPIRATION

The Sun Also Rises by Ernest Hemingway (1926). The American expat Lost Generation is on display in Hemingway's first novel. Protagonist Jake Barnes spends time in Paris café society amongst other expats, playing tennis, drinking heavily, and engaging in a love affair with Lady Brett Ashley. Later, Jake and friends travel to Pamplona to participate in the Festival of San Fermín, made famous for its running of the bulls.

1½ ounces (45 ml) tequila

1 ounce (30 ml) orange juice

½ ounce (15 ml) fresh lime juice

½ ounce (15 ml) triple sec

2 dashes habanero bitters

¾ ounce (22 ml) grenadine

Orange half-wheel, for garnishing

1. In a shaker filled with ice, combine the tequila, orange juice, lime juice, triple sec, and bitters.
2. Cover and shake thoroughly until chilled.
3. Strain into a rocks glass filled with ice.
4. Slowly pour the grenadine over the back of a barspoon, making sure the spoon is in direct contact with the glass. The grenadine should settle at the bottom of the glass and create a layered effect.
5. Garnish with the orange half-wheel.

VOL.
III.

TOME 2
VOL. II.

HOW *to* BUILD *a* BOOK CLUB *That* LASTS

We've been in the same book club since 2011. When Erin joined, it was only a few months old, started by a mutual friend who wanted to read more, and was interested in meeting new people. After fifteen years, we've learned a lot about keeping a book club running consistently. Here's how our book club works, and some helpful tips for keeping your own book club running smoothly.

SOME THINGS TO CONSIDER BEFORE YOU GET STARTED

There's no right or wrong way to run a book club; however, it works best if everyone is on the same page about what the expectations are.

WHAT IS THE GOAL OF YOUR BOOK CLUB?

Setting expectations ahead of time is helpful to current and future members. Does this book club expect everyone to read the book in full and come prepared with annotated copies and questions for the group? Or is it a bit more lax, with a primary goal of socializing and imbibing?

SCHEDULING

In the beginning of our book club, we used a digital calendar tool to try to find a mutually agreeable date for all book club members over email. This proved problematic, particularly over the years as our schedules got busier. We also used to change the date of the book club if one member couldn't attend, but rescheduling a large group of people was always a nightmare. Now, we pick the date of the next meeting at the end of the current meeting. Everyone pulls out their phones, and we try to pick a date that works well for the majority of the group. If someone can't make it, they can't make it, and we'll see them at the next one!

You could also set the schedule in advance. Perhaps it's the first [pick a day] of the month. You could also schedule out quarterly or set dates for the entire year upfront. It depends on the needs of the group, so maybe a poll ahead of time would work best to alleviate scheduling pressures and frustrations.

ADMIN

We highly recommend picking one person (in the case of our book club, it's Erin) to volunteer as book club "secretary." This person sends a digital calendar invite to all members of the book club, reminders, links to where the book can be purchased (hello, bookclubbar.com!) as well as scanning availability at the local library, or links to audiobook copies. This will eliminate confusion in the instance of books with similar titles, or around those harder-to-find books.

ADDING OR REMOVING BOOK CLUB MEMBERS

We've had both a consistent core group of members over the fifteen years of our book club and a plethora of new members who have joined or left for various reasons (work schedules, moving, time constraints, etc.). While plenty of our book club members are friends outside the group (or in our case, married), seeking out additional members with varied interests and perspectives is essential. Depth of opinions and life experience will only serve to enrich your book discussions.

BOOK CLUB *Models*

We always enjoy learning how other book clubs run. Below are a few models we've encountered over the years that your group might consider.

OPEN DISCUSSION

This loose format is how our book club is run. Typically, the person who picked the book for that month will kick off the conversation with their broad thoughts and initial reaction to the book, and we let the discussion flow from there. We interrupt each other, side conversations happen, we argue and laugh a lot. Tangents occur, and we need to refocus, but the book does indeed get discussed! In our book club, many of the members finish the book on time (some the day-of), though not everyone. Spoilers are permitted for those who didn't finish. We often read the book in either print or audio format, which adds an extra layer to the discussion. In addition, because we've read so many books at this point, discussions can hearken back to other books we've read, and we do end up talking about so much more than just the current month's book selection.

FACILITATED DISCUSSION

A little more structured, this type of book club really focuses on the text. Group members, or one appointed leader, come prepared with background information, discussion questions, and analysis. Pages are tabbed, highlighted, or dog-eared. The vibe is more upper-level English class and less "wine club."

BOOKSTORE-RUN CLUBS

Many independent bookstores, such as Book Club Bar, run their own in-house book clubs. We offer several genres (romance, philosophy, general fiction, and poetry) and rely on staff members with expertise or interest in those genres to facilitate. As not everyone comes into the book club meeting knowing other people, it's a great place to meet people with common interests.

MOVIE PAIRING

Some book clubs pair a book with its film adaptation. Everyone reads the book, then they watch the movie together, and analyze the adaptation.

WINE CLUB

We all have heard about this type of book club, and there's no shame in it! This format of book club is mostly just socializing and enjoying a few drinks, with the occasional discussion of a book. Feel free to use this book as your guide!

HOW *to* PICK *a* BOOK

There's a lot of pressure surrounding a book club pick. You're choosing how to spend your free time (and how others will spend theirs!). We have some suggestions to help take the edge off.

FIRST, MANAGE EXPECTATIONS

Setting some parameters ahead of time will help make sure everyone is on the same page (so to speak). Here are some helpful questions to discuss with the group:

- What genres of books do you want to read?
- If sticking to fiction: broad fiction, or genre fiction?
- If reading nonfiction: biography, memoir, or history? Do you want to stick to a particular subject or time period?
- Do you want to read plays or poetry?
- Do you want to read works in translation?
- Are there any authors or genres you will avoid?
- Do you want to stick to a certain page length or book size?
- Are you reading prize winners only, or following a celebrity book club list?

Of course, there are exceptions to everything. (Our book club infamously read Stephen King's *It*, a whopping 1,100 pages, and it took months. Reading the full collection of Murakami's *1Q84* nearly broke us.)

THEN, DECIDE ON A METHOD

These are a few of the book selection methods we know work well.

- **ROTATING BOOK SELECTION:** This is what our book club does. We take turns picking the book, rotating monthly. When a new member joins, they get added to the bottom of the rotation list, so by the time it's their turn to pick, they have attended the book club for months and have a sense of what type of book might elicit an interesting discussion. We don't allow vetoes of a pick, so we are making a commitment to read whatever that person chooses. The person selecting the book may or may not have already read the book.

- **GROUP LEADER / FACILITATOR:** Sometimes a group might be lopsided in terms of how much reading the members do. One person might be an avid reader, and exposed to new titles and authors frequently, while others may only read within their book club. In this instance, a group leader might be appointed to research and make book selections for the group, and to facilitate discussion.

- **VOTING / PITCHING:** Many book clubs operate democratically, with each member submitting a book to be read, and members conducting a simple vote to decide the book selection. In one book club we know, the book club breaks for months at a time. In their off time, they read multiple books, and upon reconvening "pitch" their favorites to be chosen by the book club. The members then vote on which books they are going to read and plan out the rest of the year based on these pre-selected titles.

HOSTING *and* THEME SUGGESTIONS

When hosting your book club, there are many things you can do to facilitate a memorable and fun event. Our obvious suggestion is to pick a themed cocktail or mocktail, but here are some other ideas for throwing your own book club meeting.

CONCEPTUAL DECOR OR COSTUMES

Transform your home or meeting space to reflect the time or atmosphere of the book. Try seashells for a beach read, or classic 1980s attire for a novel set in that decade. If the book takes place in the West, don your boots or cowboy hat!

GAME NIGHT

Prepare a simple round of trivia with questions about the book. This can spark a discussion about certain elements of the story that may have been overlooked in general discussion.

THEMED SNACKS

Everybody loves a cookie with a character, image, or joke from the book. Make a snack that sparks everybody's ideas and satisfies their sweet tooth.

PLAY-ACTING

Pick a scene of dialogue from the book that is especially striking, funny, or strange. Assign each person a role to read and act it out.

RELEVANT MUSIC

One of the most important components of a party atmosphere is the music. If your book is set in a specific time period or place, put together a playlist to reflect that mood.

SEASONAL SELECTIONS

Spring is a time of renewal, so a book about rebirth is an apt pick for April. If it's October, maybe a spooky pick is calling you. In the summertime, perhaps you'd enjoy a beach read and a meeting outdoors.

LITERARY PASTIMES

Provide an activity for your guests inspired by a character's interests or hobbies. One might include a flower bar for a florist, small canvases to paint for an artist, or a simple recipe to make for a passionate cook.

GET CRAFTY

A fun option for any title is for readers to create literary-themed crafts. This might include bookmarks, coasters for your Book Club Bar cocktail, or old-fashioned, brown paper bag book covers decorated with your own art.

OUR *Top 100* BOOK CLUB PICKS

Here are some books that are sure to spark a great conversation and debate.

Half of a Yellow Sun
Chimamanda Ngozi Adichie (2006)

The White Tiger
Aravind Adiga (2008)

Martyr!
Kaveh Akbar (2024)

Rashomon and Seventeen Other Stories
Ryunosuke Akutagawa (1915)

Sunset Park
Paul Auster (2010)

Cassandra at the Wedding
Dorothy Baker (1962)

Anxious People
Fredrik Backman (2019)

On the Calculation of Volume (Book I)
Solvej Balle (2024)

The Last Unicorn
Peter S. Beagle (1968)

The Sellout
Paul Beatty (2015)

The Postcard
Anne Berest (2021)

Rubyfruit Jungle
Rita Mae Brown (1973)

Ham on Rye
Charles Bukowski (1982)

The Master and Margarita
Mikhail Bulgakov (1940)

Dawn
Octavia Butler (1987)

Nights at the Circus
Angela Carter (1984)

Moonglow
Michael Chabon (2016)

The Membranes
Chi Ta-wei (2021)

Exhalation
Ted Chiang (2019)

Disgrace
J. M. Coetzee (1999)

Monstrilio
Gerardo Sámano Córdova (2023)

Razorblade Tears
S.A. Cosby (2021)

Dark Matter
Blake Crouch (2016)

Break It Down
Lydia Davis (1986)

Lightning Rods
Helen DeWitt (2011)

Play It As It Lays
Joan Didion (1970)

The End of Vandalism
Tom Drury (1994)

Manhattan Beach
Jennifer Egan (2017)

Girl, Woman, Other
Bernardine Evaristo (2019)

Erasure
Percival Everett (2001)

The Sound and the Fury
William Faulkner (1929)

The Corrections
Jonathan Franzen (2001)

Good Omens
Neil Gaiman and Terry Pratchett (1990)

An Untamed State
Roxane Gay (2014)

The Great Transition
Nick Fuller Googins (2023)

Less
Andrew Sean Greer (2017)

Homegoing
Yaa Gyasi (2016)

The Midnight Library
Matt Haig (2020)

Asymmetry
Lisa Halliday (2018)

I Who Have Never Known Men
Jacqueline Harpman (1995)

Strangers on a Train
Patricia Highsmith (1950)

A Brief History of Seven Killings
Marlon James (2014)

An American Marriage
Tayari Jones (2018)

Breasts and Eggs
Mieko Kawakami (2019)

Small Things Like These
Claire Keegan (2020)

Man Walks Into a Room
Nicole Krauss (2002)

Immortality
Milan Kundera (1990)

The Flamethrowers
Rachel Kushner (2013)

The Left Hand of Darkness
Ursula K. Le Guin (1987)

Luster
Raven Leilani (2020)

Chronic City
Jonathan Lethem (2009)

Prophet Song
Paul Lynch (2023)

The Association of Small Bombs
Karan Mahajan (2016)

The Great Believers
Rebecca Makkai (2018)

Wolf Hall
Hilary Mantel (2009)

Love in the Time of Cholera
Gabriel García Márquez (1985)

The Tsar of Love and Techno
Anthony Marra (2015)

The Good Lord Bird
James McBride (2013)

Let the Great World Spin
Colum McCann (2009)

Bright Lights, Big City
Jay McInerny (1984)

The City and The City
China Mieville (2009)

Who Will Run the Frog Hospital?
Lorrie Moore (1994)

Beloved
Toni Morrison (1987)

The Bee Sting
Paul Murray (2023)

The Fuck-Up
Arthur Nersesian (1997)

The Sympathizer
Viet Thanh Nguyen (2015)

Ordinary Human Failings
Megan Nolan (2023)

Vurt
Jeff Noon (1993)

Made for Love
Alissa Nutting (2017)

Hamnet
Maggie O'Farrell (2020)

A Tale for the Time Being
Ruth Ozeki (2013)

Commonwealth
Ann Patchett (2016)

Lush Life
Richard Price (2008)

The End of Drum-Time
Hanna Pylväinen (2023)

The Crying of Lot 49
Thomas Pynchon (1965)

Empire Falls
Richard Russo (2001)

Extremely Loud and Incredibly Close
Jonathan Safran Foer (2005)

Lincoln in the Bardo
George Saunders (2012)

Where'd You Go, Bernadette
Maria Semple (2012)

The Book of M
Peng Shepherd (2018)

Super Sad True Love Story
Gary Shteyngart (2011)

Afterparties
Anthony Veasna So (2021)

Station Eleven
Emily St. John Mandel (2014)

Cheat Day
Liv Stratman (2021)

Shuggie Bain
Douglas Stuart (2020)

The Kitchen God's Wife
Amy Tan (2006)

Brooklyn
Colm Tóibín (2009)

Drive Your Plow Over the Bones of the Dead
Olga Tokarczuk (2019)

A Confederacy of Dunces
John Kennedy Toole (1980)

The Lincoln Highway
Amor Towles (2021)

Brother of the More Famous Jack
Barbara Trapido (1982)

Rejection
Tony Tulathimutte (2024)

The Safekeep
Yael van der Wouden (2024)

Cutting for Stone
Abraham Verghese (2009)

Slaughterhouse Five
Kurt Vonnegut (1969)

The Underground Railroad
Colson Whitehead (2016)

Nothing to See Here
Kevin Wilson (2019)

The Easter Parade
Richard Yates (1976)

Nightbitch
Rachel Yoder (2021)

The Shadow of the Wind
Carlos Ruiz Zafón (2005)

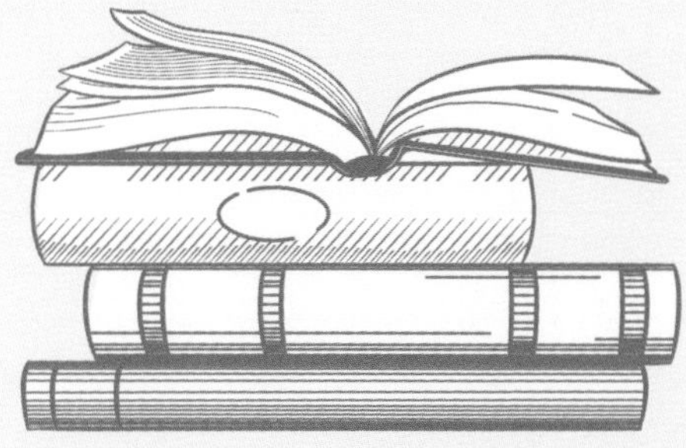

INDEX

A

absinthe
  If Bourbon Street Could Talk, 101
  Leave the World Behind, 79
  Nightingale Nectar, 105
absinthe spritz
  Dr. Frankenstein's Corpse Reviver No. 2, 75
  Heathcliff's Ghost, 93
  method, 20
Aciman, André, 117, 119
activated charcoal: Mezcal Gothic, 43
Adeyemi, Tomi, 31
The Age of Innocence (Edith Wharton), 137, 159, 160–161
Alam, Rumaan, 69, 79
Alighieri, Dante, 69
All Fours (Miranda July), 25
All the Pretty Horses (Cormac McCarthy), 130
almond bitters: Donna Plum Tartt, 121
Amaretto liqueur: The Godfather of the Woods, 47
amaro: A Court of Fig and Honey, 51
And the Mountains Echoed (Khaled Hosseini), 41
Angostura bitters
  If Bourbon Street Could Talk, 101
  No Country for Old-Fashioned Men, 129
  Old Fashioned Man and the Sea, 153
  The Sage of Innocence, 159
apple cider
  The Cider House Mules, 133
  Practically Magical Margarita, 87
apple slices
  The Cider House Mules, 133
  Practically Magical Margarita, 87
Atwood, Margaret, 95, 111, 112–113
Austen, Jane, 59, 60–61
Ayer, Gertrude E., 102

B

Bak, Lissa, 11
Baldwin, David, 102
Baldwin, James, 95, 101, 102–103
Bardem, Javier, 130
basil leaves: One Italian Summer Spritz, 57
Beach Read (Emily Henry), 65
de Beauvoir, Simone, 137, 141, 142–143
blackberries: Lessons in Chambord, 37
black pepper
  Children of Blood and Virgin Mary, 31
  In Cold Bloody Mary, 77
  Remarkably Bright Kraken, 109
blanco tequila: Tomorrow, and Tomorrow, and Tequila, 115
Blood Meridian (Cormac McCarthy), 130
Bloody Mary mix, batching without alcohol, 30
blueberries: Red, White, & Royal Blueberry, 63
Book Club Bar, 10–11, 22, 53, 91, 157, 169
book clubs
  administration of, 167
  book selection, 170–171
  bookstore-run clubs, 169
  early considerations, 166
  "facilitated discussion" format, 168
  game night, 172
  goal of, 166
  member coordination, 167
  movie pairings, 169
  music, 173
  "open discussion" format, 168
  scheduling, 166–167
  seasonal selections, 173
  snacks, 172
  theme suggestions, 172–173
  wine clubs, 169
bourbon
  If Bourbon Street Could Talk, 101
  Like Whiskey for Chocolate, 125
  No Country for Old-Fashioned Men, 129
  Old Fashioned Man and the Sea, 153
Bridgerton series (Julia Quinn), 55
Brolin, Josh, 130
Brontë, Emily, 93
Brooks, Mel, 75
brown sugar: Sage Brown Sugar Simple Syrup, 159
Buckley, William F., 102, 103
Butterfly Pea Blossom Tea: Violet's Elixir, 67

C

Call Me by Your Name (André Aciman), 117, 119
Call Me by Your Nectar, 119
Campari
  Coffee-Infused Campari, 151
  My Brilliant Ferrari, 127
  Tomorrow, and Tomorrow, and Tequila, 115
Capote, Truman, 69, 77
cardamom bitters
  Feminine Mezcal Mystique, 145
  No Country for Old-Fashioned Men, 129
le Carré, John, 80
Casino Royale (Ian Fleming), 80
celery
  Children of Blood and Virgin Mary, 31
  In Cold Bloody Mary, 77
Chambord liqueur: Lessons in Chambord, 37
charcoal: Mezcal Gothic, 43
Chartreuse liqueur
  overview, 39
  A Thousand Splendid Rums, 39
cherries
  Dirty Shirley Jackson, 83
  Like Whiskey for Chocolate, 125
  Where the Crawdads Bounce, 45
cherry vodka: Where the Crawdads Bounce, 45
Children of Blood and Bone (Tomi Adeyemi), 31
Children of Blood and Virgin Mary (NA), 31
chocolate bitters
  Like Whiskey for Chocolate, 125
  Madame Boulevardier, 151
chocolate syrup: Like Whiskey for Chocolate, 125
chocolate whiskey: Like Whiskey for Chocolate, 125
Christie, Agatha, 69, 71, 72–73
Christie, Archibald "Archie," 72
The Cider House Mules, 133
The Cider House Rules (John Irving), 117, 133

cinnamon: Practically Magical Margarita, 87
Cinnamon Simple Syrup
The Cider House Mules, 133
The Pineapple Rum Diary, 135
recipe, 133
cinnamon sticks
The Cider House Mules, 133
Cinnamon Simple Syrup, 133
Practically Magical Margarita, 87
Classic Martini, 79
Codman, Ogden, Jr., 160
Coffee-Infused Campari
Madame Boulevardier, 151
recipe, 151
cognac: Nightingale Nectar, 105
A Court of Fig and Honey, 51
A Court of Thorns and Roses (Sarah J. Maas), 25, 49, 51, 52
cranberry juice
The Handmaid's Cocktail, 111
Sex on the North Bear Shores Beach, 65
A Virgin Suicide Shaker (NA), 99
Where the Crawdads Bounce, 45
crema, 71
Crescent City series (Sarah J. Maas), 53
Crucial Instances (Edith Wharton), 160
cucumber
Marinated Cucumber, 155
One Flew Over the Cucumber's Nest, 155
Remarkably Bright Kraken, 109
Cullen, Countee, 102
curaçao: The Deluge, 139

D

De Beauvoir 75, 141
The Decoration of Houses (Edith Wharton and Ogden Codman Jr.), 160
The Deluge, 139
Depp, Johnny, 135
Dirty Martini, 79
Dirty Shirley Jackson, 83
The Divine Comedy (Dante Alighieri), 69
Donna Plum Tartt, 121
Double Persephone (Margaret Atwood), 113
Doyle, Sir Arthur Conan, 72
Dracula (Bram Stoker), 69
Drambuie liqueur: Smoke & Mirrors, 81
Dr. Frankenstein's Corpse Reviver No. 2, 75
Dry Martini, 79
dry vermouth
Leave the World Behind, 79
Tomorrow, and Tomorrow, and Tequila, 115
The Duke and I (Julia Quinn), 55

E

Earl Grey Simple Syrup
De Beauvoir 75, 141
The Picture of Dorian Earl Grey, 157
recipe, 141
East of Eden (John Steinbeck), 148
Ellis, Bret Easton, 122
espresso: Murder on the Orient Espresso Martini, 71
Esquivel, Laura, 125
Ethan Frome (Edith Wharton), 160
Eugenides, Jeffrey, 95, 99
Evers, Medgar, 103

F

Fear and Loathing in Las Vegas (Hunter S. Thompson), 135
Fee Foam
Donna Plum Tartt, 121
Feminine Mezcal Mystique, 145
overview, 121
Feminine Mezcal Mystique, 145
The Feminine Mystique (Betty Friedan), 145
Fernet-Branca: My Brilliant Ferrari, 127
Ferrante, Elena, 127
Fig and Honey Syrup
A Court of Fig and Honey, 51
recipe, 51
Fighting France: From Dunkerque to Belfort (Edith Wharton), 160
fig spread: Fig and Honey Syrup, 51
The Fire Next Time (James Baldwin), 103
Flaubert, Gustave, 137, 151
Fleming, Ian, 80
Fourth Wing (Rebecca Yarros), 49, 67
Frankenstein (Mary Shelley), 69, 75
Frank's Red Hot Sauce
Children of Blood and Virgin Mary, 31
In Cold Bloody Mary, 77
Friedan, Betty, 137, 142, 145

G

Garmus, Bonnie, 37
A Gentleman in Moscow (Amor Towles), 25, 27, 28
A Gentleman in Moscow Mule, 27
Gibson, 79
gin
Classic Martini, 79
A Court of Fig and Honey, 51
De Beauvoir 75, 141
The Deluge, 139
Dirty Martini, 79
Dry Martini, 79
A Gentleman in Moscow Mule, 27
Gibson, 79
It Ends with Citrus, 35
Leave the World Behind, 79
Lessons in Chambord, 37
The Picture of Dorian Earl Grey, 157
ginger: Marinated Cucumber, 155
ginger beer
The Cider House Mules, 133
Dirty Shirley Jackson, 83
A Gentleman in Moscow Mule, 27
On Earth We're Briefly Sober (NA), 107
Giovanni's Room (James Baldwin), 102
glassware
chilling, 20
overview, 14
glitter: Violet's Elixir, 67
The Godfather of the Woods, 47
The God of the Woods (Liz Moore), 47
The Goldfinch (Donna Tartt), 123
Go Tell It on the Mountain (James Baldwin), 102
grapefruit juice
Dr. Frankenstein's Corpse Reviver No. 2, 75
Grapefruits of Wrath, 147
Heathcliff's Ghost, 93
One Italian Summer Spritz, 57
Rosemary's Baby, 89
grapefruit pieces
Dr. Frankenstein's Corpse Reviver No. 2, 75
Grapefruits of Wrath, 147
Heathcliff's Ghost, 93
The Grapes of Wrath (John Steinbeck), 137, 147, 148, 149
green olives
Children of Blood and Virgin Mary, 31
In Cold Bloody Mary, 77

grenadine
Dirty Shirley Jackson, 83
The Seven Husbands of Mary Pickford, 33
The Tequila Sun Also Rises, 163
A Virgin Suicide Shaker (NA), 99

H

habanero bitters
One Flew Over the Cucumber's Nest, 155
The Seven Husbands of Mary Pickford, 33
The Tequila Sun Also Rises, 163
habanero tincture: Mezcal Gothic, 43
Hammer, Armie, 119
The Handmaid's Cocktail, 111
The Handmaid's Tale (Margaret Atwood), 95, 111, 112
Hangsaman (Shirley Jackson), 84
Hannah, Kristin, 95, 105
Harlem Renaissance, 102
Harpman, Jaqueline, 25
The Haunting of Hill House (Shirley Jackson), 69, 84
Hawthorne strainers, 15
Heathcliff's Ghost, 93
Hemingway, Ernest, 130, 137, 153, 163
Henry, Emily, 65
Herron, Mick, 69, 81
Hoffman, Alice, 87
honey
Fig and Honey Syrup, 51
Honey Syrup, 81
Lady Whistledown's Tea, 55
Honey Syrup
On Earth We're Briefly Sober (NA), 107
recipe 81
Smoke & Mirrors, 81
Hoover, Colleen, 35
horseradish
Children of Blood and Virgin Mary, 31
In Cold Bloody Mary, 77
Hosseini, Khaled, 25, 39, 40–41
hot sauce
Children of Blood and Virgin Mary, 31
In Cold Bloody Mary, 77
Remarkably Bright Kraken, 109
The House of Mirth (Edith Wharton), 160
Hurston, Zora Neale, 137, 139

I

If Beale Street Could Talk (James Baldwin), 101
If Bourbon Street Could Talk, 101
In Cold Blood (Truman Capote), 69, 77
In Cold Bloody Mary, 77
In Glorious Battle (John Steinbeck), 148
Irving, John, 117, 133
It Ends with Citrus, 35
It Ends with Us (Colleen Hoover), 35
I Who Have Never Known Men (Jaqueline Harpman), 25

J

Jackson, Shirley, 69, 83, 84–85
jiggers, 15
Jones, Catherine Zeta, 84
Jones, Emma, 102
Jones, Tommy Lee, 130
julep strainers, 15
July, Miranda, 25

K

Kahlúa: Murder on the Orient Espresso Martini, 71
Kesey, Ken, 137, 155
Khaled Hosseini Foundation, 41
King, Martin Luther, Jr., 103
The Kite Runner (Khaled Hosseini), 25, 40

L

Lady Whistledown's Tea, 55
lavender syrup
On Earth We're Briefly Sober (NA), 107
Red, White & Royal Blueberry, 63
Violet's Elixir, 67
Leave the World Behind (Rumaan Alam), 69, 79
Lee, Harper, 77
lemon juice
Call Me by Your Nectar, 119
Children of Blood and Virgin Mary, 31
A Court of Fig and Honey, 51
De Beauvoir 75, 141
Donna Plum Tartt, 121
Dr. Frankenstein's Corpse Reviver No. 2, 75
Feminine Mezcal Mystique, 145
In Cold Bloody Mary, 77
Lady Whistledown's Tea, 55
Lessons in Chambord, 37
Nightingale Nectar, 105
One Italian Summer Spritz, 57
Pearsuasian Martini, 59
The Picture of Dorian Earl Grey, 157
Red, White & Royal Blueberry, 63
Sex on the North Bear Shores Beach (NA), 65
Violet's Elixir, 67
lemon pieces
Children of Blood and Virgin Mary, 31
If Bourbon Street Could Talk, 101
In Cold Bloody Mary, 77
Lady Whistledown's Tea, 55
Lessons in Chambord, 37
Smoke & Mirrors, 81
Violet's Elixir, 67
lemon twists
A Court of Fig and Honey, 51
De Beauvoir 75, 141
Donna Plum Tartt, 121
Feminine Mezcal Mystique, 145
The Handmaid's Cocktail, 111
Leave the World Behind, 79
Remarkably Bright Kraken, 109
Lessons in Chambord, 37
Lessons in Chemistry (Bonnie Garmus), 25, 37
Lethem, Jonathan, 122
Levin, Ira, 89
Like Water for Chocolate (Laura Esquivel), 125
Like Whiskey for Chocolate, 125
lime juice
The Deluge, 139
Dirty Shirley Jackson, 83
A Gentleman in Moscow Mule, 27
Grapefruits of Wrath, 147
The Handmaid's Cocktail, 111
Heathcliff's Ghost, 93
It Ends with Citrus, 35
On Earth We're Briefly Sober (NA), 107
One Flew Over the Cucumber's Nest, 155
The Pineapple Rum Diary, 135
Practically Magical Margarita, 87
Rosemary's Baby, 89
Sex on the North Bear Shores Beach (NA), 65
The Tequila Sun Also Rises, 163
A Thousand Splendid Rums, 39
The Thursday Murder Mezcal Margarita, 91
A Virgin Suicide Shaker (NA), 99
Where the Crawdads Bounce, 45

lime pieces
The Deluge, 139
Dirty Shirley Jackson, 83
A Gentleman in Moscow Mule, 27
Mezcal Gothic, 43
A Thousand Splendid Rums, 39
The Thursday Murder Mezcal Margarita, 91
The Lincoln Highway (Amor Towles), 29
The Little Friend (Donna Tartt), 122
"The Lottery" (Shirley Jackson), 84, 85

M

Maas, Sarah J., 25, 51, 52–53
Madame Boulevardier, 151
Madame Bovary (Gustave Flaubert), 137, 151
Maheu, René, 142
Mallowan, Max, 72–73
maple syrup
Feminine Mezcal Mystique, 145
No Country for Old-Fashioned Men, 129
maraschino cherries
Dirty Shirley Jackson, 83
Like Whiskey for Chocolate, 125
Where the Crawdads Bounce, 45
maraschino liqueur: The Seven Husbands of Mary Pickford, 33
Marinated Cucumber
One Flew Over the Cucumber's Nest, 155
recipe, 155
McCarthy, Cormac, 117, 129, 130–131
McQuiston, Casey, 63
Melville, Herman, 153
mezcal
Dr. Frankenstein's Corpse Reviver No. 2, 75
Feminine Mezcal Mystique, 145
Mezcal Gothic, 43
The Thursday Murder Mezcal Margarita, 91
Middlesex (Jeffrey Eugenides), 95
mint leaves
Grapefruits of Wrath, 147
It Ends with Citrus, 35
Mint Simple Syrup, 35
Mint Simple Syrup
Grapefruits of Wrath, 147
It Ends with Citrus, 35
recipe, 35
mixing glasses, 15
Moby-Dick (Herman Melville), 153
Moore, Liz, 47
Moss, Elizabeth, 112
And the Mountains Echoed (Khaled Hosseini), 41
The Mousetrap (Agatha Christie), 72
Murder on the Orient Espresso Martini, 71
Murder on the Orient Express (Agatha Christie), 71
The Murders in the Rue Morge (Edgar Allen Poe), 69
My Brilliant Ferrari, 127
My Brilliant Friend (Elena Ferrante), 117, 127
The Mysterious Affair at Styles (Agatha Christie), 72

N

NA (nonalcoholic) beverages
Bloody Mary mix, 30
Children of Blood and Virgin Mary, 31
On Earth We're Briefly Sober, 107
One Italian Summer Spritz, 57
Sex on the North Bear Shores Beach, 65
Neeson, Liam, 84
The Nightingale (Kristin Hannah), 95, 105
Nightingale Nectar, 105
Nizan, Paul, 142
No Country for Old-Fashioned Men, 129
No Country for Old Men (Cormac McCarthy), 117, 129, 130
Notes of a Native Son (James Baldwin), 102

O

Obama, Barack, 28
Of Mice and Men (John Steinbeck), 148
Old Fashioned Man and the Sea, 153
The Old Man and the Sea (Ernest Hemingway), 137, 153
Oldman, Gary, 81
olives, green
Children of Blood and Virgin Mary, 31
In Cold Bloody Mary, 77
On Earth We're Briefly Gorgeous (Ocean Vuong), 95, 107
On Earth We're Briefly Sober (NA), 107
One Flew Over the Cuckoo's Nest (Ken Kesey), 137, 155
One Flew Over the Cucumber's Nest, 155
One Italian Summer (Rebecca Serle), 57
One Italian Summer Spritz (NA), 57
orange bitters
Like Whiskey for Chocolate, 125
The Sage of Innocence, 159
orange juice
One Italian Summer Spritz, 57
Sex on the North Bear Shores Beach, 65
The Tequila Sun Also Rises, 163
orange pieces
Like Whiskey for Chocolate, 125
My Brilliant Ferrari, 127
One Italian Summer Spritz, 57
The Picture of Dorian Earl Grey, 157
Sex on the North Bear Shores Beach, 65
The Tequila Sun Also Rises, 163
Tomorrow, and Tomorrow, and Tequila, 115
orange twists
Madame Boulevardier, 151
Nightingale Nectar, 105
No Country for Old-Fashioned Men, 129
Old Fashioned Man and the Sea, 153
Osman, Richard, 91
Owens, Delia, 45

P

peach bitters: Old Fashioned Man and the Sea, 153
peach juice: Call Me by Your Nectar, 119
peach nectar
Call Me by Your Nectar, 119
Sex on the North Bear Shores Beach (NA), 65
peach schnapps: Sex on the North Bear Shores Beach, 65
peach syrup: Old Fashioned Man and the Sea, 153
Pear-Infused Vodka
Pearsuasian Martini, 59
recipe, 59
pears
Pear-Infused Vodka, 59
Pearsuasian Martini, 59
pepper, black
Children of Blood and Virgin Mary, 31
In Cold Bloody Mary, 77

Remarkably Bright Kraken, 109
Persuasion (Jane Austen), 59
Peychaud's Bitters: If Bourbon Street Could Talk, 101
pickle brine: Remarkably Bright Kraken, 109
The Picture of Dorian Earl Grey, 157
The Picture of Dorian Gray (Oscar Wilde), 137, 157
The Pineapple Rum Diary, 135
pineapple juice
The Pineapple Rum Diary, 135
The Seven Husbands of Mary Pickford, 33
A Virgin Suicide Shaker (NA), 99
pineapple pieces
The Pineapple Rum Diary, 135
A Virgin Suicide Shaker (NA), 99
pine liqueur
The Godfather of the Woods, 47
pistachio syrup: A Thousand Splendid Rums, 39
plum liqueur: Donna Plum Tartt, 121
Poe, Edgar Allen, 69
Porter, Bill, 102
Practically Magical Margarita, 87
Practical Magic (Alice Hoffman), 87
A Prayer for Owen Meany (John Irving), 117
Prosecco
De Beauvoir 75, 141
My Brilliant Ferrari, 127

Q

Queen Esther (John Irving), 133
Quinn, Julia, 55

R

raspberries: Sex on the North Bear Shores Beach, 65
Red, White & Royal Blueberry, 63
Red, White & Royal Blue (Casey McQuiston), 63
Regency period, 55
Reid, Taylor Jenkins, 33
Remarkably Bright Creatures (Shelby Van Pelt), 95, 109
Remarkably Bright Kraken, 109
rinsing technique, 20
The Road (Cormac McCarthy), 130
rock candy: On Earth We're Briefly Sober (NA), 107
rosemary
The Godfather of the Woods, 47
Rosemary's Baby, 89
Rosemary Simple Syrup, 89
Rosemary's Baby (Ira Levin), 89
Rosemary Simple Syrup
recipe, 89
Rosemary's Baby, 89
rose water: A Thousand Splendid Rums, 39
Rules of Civility (Amor Towles), 28, 29
rum
The Cider House Mules, 133
Lady Whistledown's Tea, 55
The Pineapple Rum Diary, 135
Remarkably Bright Kraken, 109
The Seven Husbands of Mary Pickford, 33
A Thousand Splendid Rums, 39
The Rum Diary (Hunter S. Thompson), 135
rye whiskey
Like Whiskey for Chocolate, 125
The Sage of Innocence, 159

S

Sage Brown Sugar Simple Syrup
recipe. 159
The Sage of Innocence, 159
sage leaves
Sage Brown Sugar Simple Syrup, 159
The Sage of Innocence, 159
salt
Marinated Cucumber, 155
Remarkably Bright Kraken, 109
Sage Brown Sugar Simple Syrup, 159
Sartre, Jean-Paul, 142
schnapps, peach: Sex on the North Bear Shores Beach, 65
Scotch
The Godfather of the Woods, 47
Smoke & Mirrors, 81
Scribner's Magazine, 160
Sea Prayer (Khaled Hosseini), 41
The Second Sex (Simone de Beauvoir), 142, 143
The Secret History (Donna Tartt), 117, 122
Serle, Rebecca, 57
sesame oil: Marinated Cucumber, 155
The Seven Husbands of Mary Pickford, 33
The Seven Husbands of Evelyn Hugo (Taylor Jenkins Reid), 33
Sex on the North Bear Shores Beach, 65
shakers, 15, 20
Shelley, Mary, 69, 75
Simple Syrup
Donna Plum Tartt, 121
Dr. Frankenstein's Corpse Reviver No. 2, 75
Heathcliff's Ghost, 93
If Bourbon Street Could Talk, 101
Lessons in Chambord, 37
Murder on the Orient Espresso Martini, 71
One Flew Over the Cucumber's Nest, 155
recipe, 37
Remarkably Bright Kraken, 109
The Thursday Murder Mezcal Margarita, 91
simple syrups
Cinnamon Simple Syrup, 133
Earl Grey Simple Syrup, 141
Mint Simple Syrup, 35
Rosemary Simple Syrup, 89
Sage Brown Sugar Simple Syrup, 159
Simple Syrup, 37
skewers, 15
sloe gin: Lessons in Chambord, 37
Slow Horses (Mick Herron), 69, 81
Smoke & Mirrors, 81
soda water
Grapefruits of Wrath, 147
One Italian Summer Spritz, 57
Red, White & Royal Blueberry, 63
Rosemary's Baby, 89
A Virgin Suicide Shaker (NA), 99
Where the Crawdads Bounce, 45
spiced rum
Lady Whistledown's Tea, 55
Remarkably Bright Kraken, 109
spicy tincture
overview of, 91
The Thursday Murder Mezcal Margarita, 91
"splash" measurement, 20
star anise pods
Dr. Frankenstein's Corpse Reviver No. 2, 75
Heathcliff's Ghost, 93
Smoke & Mirrors, 81
Steinbeck, Carole, 149
Steinbeck, John, 137, 147, 148–149
St. Germain liqueur: Pearsuasian Martini, 59
stirring spoons, 15
stirring technique, 21
Stoker, Bram, 69
strawberries: A Virgin Suicide Shaker (NA), 99
sugar

Cinnamon Simple Syrup, 133
Earl Grey Simple Syrup, 141
If Bourbon Street Could Talk, 101
Mint Simple Syrup, 35
Nightingale Nectar, 105
Practically Magical Margarita, 87
Rosemary Simple Syrup, 89
Simple Syrup, 37
The Sun Also Rises (Ernest Hemingway), 137, 163
sweet vermouth
Madame Boulevardier, 151
Tomorrow, and Tomorrow, and Tequila, 115

T

Tabasco: Lady Whistledown's Tea, 55
Tartt, Donna, 117, 121, 122–123
tea
Earl Grey Simple Syrup, 141
Red, White & Royal Blueberry, 63
Violet's Elixir, 67
tequila
Grapefruits of Wrath, 147
Heathcliff's Ghost, 93
One Flew Over the Cucumber's Nest, 155
Practically Magical Margarita, 87
Rosemary's Baby, 89
The Tequila Sun Also Rises, 163
Tomorrow, and Tomorrow, and Tequila, 115
The Greater Inclination (Edith Wharton), 160
Their Eyes Were Watching God (Zora Neale Hurston), 137, 139
Thompson, Hunter S., 135
A Thousand Splendid Rums, 39
A Thousand Splendid Suns (Khaled Hosseini), 25, 39, 40
Throne of Glass series (Sarah J. Maas), 52
The Thursday Murder Club (Richard Osman), 91
The Thursday Murder Mezcal Margarita, 91
TIME Magazine, 103
tomato juice
Children of Blood and Virgin Mary, 31
In Cold Bloody Mary, 77
Tomorrow, and Tomorrow, and Tequila, 115
Tomorrow, and Tomorrow, and Tomorrow (Gabrielle Zevin), 95, 115
tools, 14–15
toothpicks, 15
Towles, Amor, 27, 28–29
triple sec
Dr. Frankenstein's Corpse Reviver No. 2, 75
The Handmaid's Cocktail, 111
Heathcliff's Ghost, 93
It Ends with Citrus, 35
Mezcal Gothic, 43
Nightingale Nectar, 105
Practically Magical Margarita, 87
Sex on the North Bear Shores Beach, 65
The Tequila Sun Also Rises, 163
Violet's Elixir, 67

U

Ume plum liqueur: Donna Plum Tartt, 121
UNHCR (United Nations High Commissioner for Refugees), 41

V

The Valley of Decision (Edith Wharton), 160
vanilla syrup: The Picture of Dorian Earl Grey, 157
Van Pelt, Shelby, 95, 109
vermouth
Classic Martini, 79
Dirty Martini, 79
Dry Martini, 79
Leave the World Behind, 79
Madame Boulevardier, 151
Tomorrow, and Tomorrow, and Tequila, 115
Violet's Elixir, 67
The Virgin Suicides (Jeffrey Eugenides), 95, 99
A Virgin Suicide Shaker (NA), 99
vodka
Call Me by Your Nectar, 119
Dirty Shirley Jackson, 83
Donna Plum Tartt, 121
A Gentleman in Moscow Mule, 27
The Handmaid's Cocktail, 111
In Cold Bloody Mary, 77
Murder on the Orient Espresso Martini, 71
Pear-Infused Vodka, 59
Pearsuasian Martini, 59
Red, White & Royal Blueberry, 63
Sex on the North Bear Shores Beach, 65
Violet's Elixir, 67
Where the Crawdads Bounce, 45
Vuong, Ocean, 95, 107

W

We Have Always Lived in the Castle (Shirley Jackson), 84
Weil, Simone, 142
Westmacott, Mary, 73
Wharton, Edith, 137, 159, 160–161
Wharton, Edward, 160
Where the Crawdads Bounce, 45
Where the Crawdads Sing (Delia Owens), 25, 45
whipped cream
Call Me by Your Nectar, 119
crema, 71
whiskey
Like Whiskey for Chocolate, 125
Madame Boulevardier, 151
white rum
The Seven Husbands of Mary Pickford, 33
A Thousand Splendid Rums, 39
Wilde, Oscar, 137, 157
Wisconsin Bloody Mary, 76
Wise, Robert, 84
Worcestershire Sauce
Children of Blood and Virgin Mary, 31
In Cold Bloody Mary, 77
The World According to Garp (John Irving), 117
Wright, Richard, 102
Wuthering Heights (Emily Brontë), 92, 93

X

X, Malcom, 103

Y

Yarros, Rebecca, 67

Z

Zevin, Gabrielle, 95, 115
Zirbenz pine liqueur
The Godfather of the Woods, 47
overview of, 47

ACKNOWLEDGMENTS

To our parents, Elizabeth and Bill Neary and Margi and Jonathan Esten, who did not bat an eye when we told them we wanted to open a brick-and-mortar store in one of the toughest markets in the world. Their belief in our little-to-no retail and minimal hospitality experience buoyed our confidence beyond measure. Without it, we may have second-guessed ourselves out of ever opening Book Club Bar.

To our friends and family in New York and around the world, thank you for being our biggest cheerleaders: spreading the word, telling your friends, buying books from us, and consistently showing up.

To our staff of Book Club Bar, past and present: a sincere thank you. The success of Book Club Bar can directly be attributed to the people behind the bar. It takes a unique skill set to work in hospitality, with all that entails, while also working in books. The ability to shake a mean cocktail and whip up some latte art while giving the perfect book recommendation is no small feat.

A special thank you to Lissa Bak, whose boundless creativity and ceaseless ability to come up with a bookish pun has contributed so significantly to the cocktails of this book, and in the success of the cocktail program at Book Club Bar. Thank you to Joe Demes who helped to perfect and style the beautiful cocktails photographed here. Thank you to Nicole, Kristy, and the team at Quarto for seeing something in our little bookstore they believed was worth sharing far and wide.

To our beloved East Village community: Thank you for embracing Book Club Bar. For being weird, interesting, creative, and keeping us on our toes. We love it here.

ABOUT *the* AUTHORS

Erin Neary is originally from Brookfield, Wisconsin. After finishing college and graduate school, she moved to New York City in 2011, where she worked in nonprofit development and in marketing for tech start-ups before deciding to make the leap into retail bookselling and hospitality. With her husband, Nat Esten, she founded Book Club Bar in 2019. When she's not reading alongside their cat, Bruce, Erin enjoys running marathons and traveling. She lives in New York.

Nat Esten is a musician who co-owns Book Club Bar with his wife, Erin Neary. When not at the shop, he can often be found playing drums in the Saved by the '90s cover band. He is a lover of the Boston Red Sox and a doer of crossword puzzles. He lives and will probably die in New York.

First published in 2026 by Epic Ink,
an imprint of The Quarto Group
135 West 36th Street, 13th Floor,
New York, NY 10018, USA
(212) 779-4972
www.Quarto.com

EEA Representation, WTS Tax d.o.o.,
Žanova ulica 3, 4000 Kranj, Slovenia.
www.wts-tax.si

Epic Ink titles are also available at discount for retail, wholesale, promotional, and bulk purchase. For details, contact the special sales manager by email at specialsales@quarto.com or by mail at The Quarto Group, Attn: Special Sales Manager, 100 Cummings Center, Suite 265D Beverly, MA 01915 USA.

10 9 8 7 6 5 4 3 2 1

ISBN: 978-1-57715-909-4

Digital edition published in 2026
eISBN: 978-1-57715-910-0

Library of Congress Control Number: 2026934183

Group Publisher: Rage Kindelsperger
Senior Acquiring Editor: Nicole James
Creative Director: Laura Drew
Senior Art Director: Marisa Kwek
Managing Editor: Cara Donaldson
Photography: Sheneur Menaker
Cover and Interior Design: Laura Klynstra
Adobe Stock: 4, 12–13
Shutterstock: 23, 96–97, 164–165

Printed in Huizhou City, Guangdong, China TT052026